W9-ARH-111

Readers and reviewers offer praise
for Allison Bottke's first Setting Boundaries™ book,
Setting Boundaries™ with Your Adult Children...

"No one knows the pain of dealing with adult children who have lost their way better than the parents of those without boundaries. Sometimes it feels as though the setting of these boundaries is more difficult than living with the anxiety, stress, and heartache, but that's not so. Allison Bottke, writing through her own hurt and experience, has compiled a masterpiece of advice. She doesn't just tell you or show you how it's done. She walks along beside you."

Eva Marie and **Jessica Everson**
authors of *Sex, Lies, and the Media*
and *Sex, Lies, and High School*

"Lack of boundaries with adult children is a worldwide epidemic with catastrophic consequences. Allison not only shares her experience as a parent who has traveled this painful road but also gives readers concrete tools to stop the insanity and start living a life of hope and healing. *Setting Boundaries with Your Adult Children* is destined to be the official resource of hope for countless parents and grandparents."

Heather Gemmen Wilson
author of *Startling Beauty: My Journey
from Rape to Restoration*

"Allison Bottke has stepped forward in a courageous, straight-from-the-heart manner and dealt with an issue that has plagued parents since the dawn of time: setting (and enforcing) boundaries for rebellious adult children. Having been not only a parent but also a pastor who faced this issue countless times, I am excited to see that a mother who has wrestled with demons to see her child delivered has written a heartfelt yet practical book of advice and encouragement that will bless each and every one who reads it."

Kathi Macias
author of 20 books, including
Mothers of the Bible Speak to Mothers Today

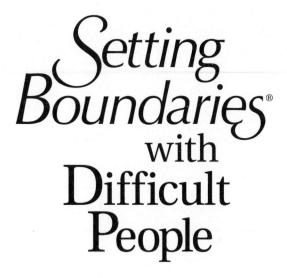

Setting Boundaries® with Difficult People

ALLISON BOTTKE

HARVEST HOUSE PUBLISHERS
EUGENE, OREGON

All Scripture quotations are taken from The Holy Bible, *New International Version® NIV®*. Copyright © 1973, 1978, 1984, 2011 by Biblica, Inc.™ Used by permission. All rights reserved worldwide.

This book contains stories in which the author has changed people's names and some details of their situations in order to protect their privacy.

Published in association with the literary agency of The Steve Laube Agency, LLC, 5025 N. Central Ave., #635, Phoenix, Arizona 85912.

Cover by Garborg Design Works, Savage, Minnesota

SETTING BOUNDARIES is a registered trademark of The Hawkins Children's LLC. Harvest House Publishers, Inc. is the exclusive licensee of the federally registered trademark SETTING BOUNDARIES.

SETTING BOUNDARIES® WITH DIFFICULT PEOPLE
Copyright © 2011 by Allison Bottke
Published by Harvest House Publishers
Eugene, Oregon 97402
www.harvesthousepublishers.com

Library of Congress Cataloging-in-Publication Data
   Bottke, Allison.
   Setting boundaries with difficult people / Allison Bottke.
      p. cm.
   Includes bibliographical references (p.).
   ISBN 978-0-7369-2696-6 (pbk.)
   ISBN 978-0-7369-4134-1 (eBook)
   1. Interpersonal conflict—Religious aspects—Christianity. 2. Interpersonal relations—Religious aspects—Christianity. I. Title.
   BV4597.53.C58B53 2011
   241'.67—dc23

                    2011018972

All rights reserved. No part of this publication may be reproduced, stored in a retrieval system, or transmitted in any form or by any means—electronic, mechanical, digital, photocopy, recording, or any other—except for brief quotations in printed reviews, without the prior permission of the publisher.

Printed in the United States of America

To the special faith-filled women
God has placed in my life.

Your love, support, encouragement,
and prayers have changed me.
The blessing of your friendship has changed my life.

I thank God for you.

Sharon Hill
Suellen Roberts
Nancy Robinson
Donna Skell
Thelma Wells

I love those who love me,
and those who seek me find me.
PROVERBS 8:17

Contents

Foreword

by Karol Ladd

As much as we would love to be surrounded by kind, refreshing, easy-going people without any issues, in reality we will always have some difficult people in our lives. Coworkers, family members, neighbors, or even cashiers at the checkout line may annoy, intrude, overwhelm, hurt, or simply bring us down by their negativity. The question is not how to avoid all difficult people, but rather how to set wise and healthy boundaries so we can respond to them in a positive way.

The good news is, we have a choice. We can choose to let difficult people rob us of our joy and drain us of our strength, or we can choose to set loving guidelines to protect ourselves as well as those around us. Using biblical truths and keen insight, Allison Bottke provides us with the tools we need to carefully set boundaries and maintain our sanity.

I have admired Allison for many years as both a colleague and a friend. She is open, honest, and real with people—no pretense. She's astute and encouraging, and she tells it like it is. That's why I like her, and that's why I like her writing style. Her books are filled with powerful and practical insight as well as engaging illustrations, personal stories, and memorable quotes. As you read this book, you'll be encouraged and uplifted by her witty and wise personality, which engages you on each page. You will also be helped and strengthened in making loving decisions regarding the challenging people in your life. Allison will show you that you can set boundaries in a way that honors both you and your difficult person.

It's time to stop the frustration you feel when you are around "sandpaper" people or difficult loved ones. It's time to stop allowing them to dictate your life. It's time to move forward with positive steps of action using loving boundaries to help you do it. As Allison puts it, stop the insanity. Start making positive and purposeful choices. Allow Allison to lead you to respectful and healthy solutions in dealing with the difficult people in your life.

Introduction

I'd like to believe that most difficult people do not intentionally set out to be difficult, that the people who cause us pain don't wake up every morning and say, "Today I'm going to be as difficult as humanly possible and make life miserable for so-and-so." Nonetheless, here's the rub: Regardless of their intent, they often make us uncomfortable and sometimes make life virtually unbearable.

For that reason, we can and should set healthy boundaries with the difficult people in our lives. Yet too often, we ignore the need to do so because we don't want to be misunderstood or because we want to be good Christians. We simply wait passively, letting the chips fall where they may. Or worse, we respond emotionally and aggressively, protecting ourselves at all costs. Either way, we are continually putting out fires instead of preventing them in the first place. If only we could change the difficult people in our lives!

Are there difficult people in your life who frequently disrupt your peace of mind and rob you of joy? If so, what makes them difficult? Is it something they do or don't do? Something they say or don't say? Or do they merely need to walk into the room to make your blood pressure rise?

In her book *Living Successfully with Screwed-Up People*, Elizabeth Brown offers sound advice on the relationships in our lives that make us feel crazy.

Unfortunately, difficult relationships are like swamps. In a swamp your vision is obscured by vines, alligators, snakes, and mosquitoes. Screwed-up relationships are mired in muck and swamped by chaos. So much is going on, you don't know how to find solid ground. About the time you begin to wade out of a period of turmoil, a snake bites or an alligator threatens and you lose your footing. Your struggle for self-preservation so occupies you that you are unable to analyze the source of your problems. You wonder: Am I responsible for all this chaos? Or is the person who drives me crazy truly messed up and responsible for the havoc?[1]

An Uncomfortable Truth

This book explores an uncomfortable truth regarding setting boundaries with the difficult people in your life: Your focus cannot be on changing them—it must be on changing the way you respond to them.

The responsibility for change is *yours*.

If you're struggling with difficult people, if you're turned inside out and living from one crisis to the next in pain, fear, anger, or frustration because of the behavior and choices of others, there's a strong probability that you're making some poor choices yourself. Please don't misunderstand—I'm not blaming you for the problems you may be having with difficult people. They are very likely behaving in reprehensible or inappropriate ways. But their actions, no matter how atrocious, do not dictate your response. How you respond to them can make all the difference—and that's what I want to address in these pages.

Therefore, the primary goal of this book is to help you identify the role you play in your relationships with difficult people and empower you to make new choices—choices that will bring freedom and forever change the story of your life regardless of whether the difficult people around you ever change one iota.

Here's something else to consider: Could God be using difficult people or difficult situations in our lives to help us grow in wisdom and knowledge? To help us be the people He wants us to be? Could it be that we have difficult people in our lives because we ourselves are difficult? Because we haven't quite learned how to communicate effectively?

Two Little Words

If, like me, you've had to deal with a difficult person for several years or more, it's very likely that even after all this time, you still have great difficulty saying and *meaning* two simple words: *yes* and *no*. Other factors are also part of the equation, but these two simple words form the rudimentary basis of setting healthy boundaries.

How we speak these words is important. Most professional counselors and therapists tell us that our communication is taken far more seriously when we can speak calmly—when we are in a rational state of mind—than when we yell in the heat of an emotional moment, when we've been pushed to the edge, and when our nerves are exposed.

To minimize frustration, it will be useful to remember that learning how to set and communicate healthy boundaries is an organic process that ebbs and flows and challenges us time and again as we're confronted by new people, new situations, new challenges, and new seasons of our own growth. Just when we think we've gotten the boundary thing down, a new situation or relationship sends us into that place of insanity where nothing makes sense, where our sure footing is yanked out from under us.

My own experience is evidence of that. This is the third Setting Boundaries book I've written, and I have to admit, there are still times when I have trouble getting it right. I still sometimes have difficulty knowing how and when to say yes and no. Occasionally I react emotionally and completely forget to practice what I preach. That's the funny thing about being human—until we're with God in heaven, we're never-ending works in progress who try, fail, and sometimes succeed. Even so, we must keep on facing the challenges presented by the difficult people God has placed in our paths.

Doing so can save our lives—at least emotionally if not physically. Difficult people can harm us if we don't have a strategy to deal with them. They can threaten us like quicksand—those hidden places that on the surface look safe but eventually suck us in, threatening our very lives. Some of our relationships are like that, and we've got to be able to identify those quicksand relationships before we step into them. Or once we're confronted with them, we need to know how to safely escape.

If you have a challenging relationship with a difficult person, *Setting Boundaries with Difficult People* will help you determine whether a lack of healthy boundaries could be the cause. It will help you see why appropriate boundaries protect both parties. It's a way to stay on alert and face problems early on so that nothing will be allowed to fester and destroy your life, your peace of mind, your sanity. You'll learn my six steps that use the acronym SANITY—valuable tools you can use to adjust any difficult relationship that threatens to hold you in bondage and rob you of peace and joy.

A Critical Truth

As odd as it may sound, I've come to realize that setting healthy boundaries is first and foremost about love—the love God has for us, the love He wants us to have for our own lives, and the love He wants us to share with others. *Setting Boundaries with Difficult People* will help you see that boundaries are biblical—that in His compassionate love for us, even Jesus set boundaries.

We can't control the way others treat us, but this book will show you how to tell them, in a positive and productive manner, how you feel about being treated poorly. Even more important, it will bring you closer to the God who wants nothing more than to hold you in the palm of His hand and love and protect you regardless of your circumstances.

As with my previous books in this series, I invite readers of all faiths to learn how to set healthy boundaries and find SANITY in seemingly out-of-control and insane situations. However, I wrote this book unapologetically from my Christian perspective and worldview. I believe that any enduring solution will include a firm trust in God. Long ago I discovered that God knows our pain and has provided not only a way of hope and healing but also guidelines for what He expects of us. God is the original designer of boundaries.

Whether your situation concerns a spouse or ex-spouse, in-law, boss, coworker, family member, neighbor, or friend, if anyone has threatened to steal your peace and joy, it's time to take back your life. With the proper mind-set and the help of an awesome God who truly loves you, you can find freedom from the bondage of difficult people.

The Six Steps to SANITY work and will help you get your life back. SANITY is possible, and I will help you find it.

Part 1

Get Ready…

Keeping Your Eye on the Goal

Runners who enter the Boston Marathon know that to successfully complete the race, they will have to run 42.195 kilometers (26 miles and 385 yards). No one who shows up at the starting line is unsure of the distance he or she will have to run. Likewise, we need to know our goals in relating to the difficult people in our lives. And we need to know that achieving our ultimate goal may require that we accomplish several supplementary goals along the way.

One marathoner said, "After a scare with my heart, I entered the race mostly to get in better physical shape. I wasn't sure I'd be able to run the entire 26 miles, but I knew the training would help." Another runner gave this reason for entering: "I needed to lose 60 pounds—that's really why I entered the race. If I reached that goal before race day and never ran, I would have succeeded." Another said, "I was recovering from knee surgery, and my underlying goal was to increase flexibility and strength in my legs. The race was the catalyst that kept me going, but it wasn't my ultimate goal."

In other words, even though these athletes' goal was to run 26.2 miles, they each had supplementary goals leading up to race day that were every bit as important.

Our Ultimate Goal

When setting boundaries with difficult people, the ultimate goal is *to achieve freedom from the bondage of drama, chaos, and crisis that often accompanies challenging relationships.* Whether those relationships are with difficult people, adult children, aging parents, teens, or perhaps even food, we need to keep our eye on that ultimate goal of freedom. We also need to understand that breaking free from anything requires hard work, and that means commitment, consistency, and consequences.

Remember too that our emotions will beg for attention when other peoples' hurtful behavior pushes our buttons. We have all developed our own coping responses as a result of our life experiences. For some of us, these coping responses lead to self-defeating, unhealthy life patterns that we repeat throughout our lives, and they act as roadblocks to freedom. When life situations trigger emotional responses, addressing our feelings is going to be a key factor in reaching our goal.

Our Supplementary Goals

As we work toward our ultimate goal, we want to accomplish several other goals as well: We want…

- to stop difficult people from hurting us
- to take control and stop the stress
- to become healthy and whole
- to gain clarity in our lives
- to learn new skills to enhance our relationships
- to live lives that are pleasing to God
- to find SANITY

Two Growth Options

Setting healthy boundaries isn't something we learn one time and then never have to think about it again. It's not like tying our shoes or riding a bike—processes we learn and then simply repeat the same way time after time with the same results. For many of us, setting boundaries is not that easy. But it doesn't have to be as problematic as we often make it.

Bestselling author and radio talk-show host Dr. Laura Schlessinger says we have two options when dealing with people who have caused us harm—real or imagined: "Either stand up for yourself—or move on. Those are the only two means of growth."[1]

That sounded a bit cut-and-dry to me when I first read it. Surely there are more than two options that will help us grow. Yet the more I thought about her statement, the more sense it made. Yes, there are a lot more options, but only if we want to remain stuck or stagnant. If we truly want to move forward (that is, if we want to grow) when someone has hurt us, Dr. Laura is right. We either stand up (speak up) or move on (shake it off). There really isn't anything else to do that initiates growth.

Standing up for yourself doesn't mean bulldozing your way over someone who has behaved poorly or has made choices that hurt you. Likewise, moving on doesn't mean glossing over a problem, ignoring it, or denying that something is wrong.

Both standing up and moving on are conscious decisions we must make. Learning how to stand up or move on is a vital part in gaining SANITY.

A Lesson Learned

I was sitting on the outdoor patio at a local restaurant with several friends on a beautiful fall day, enjoying good food and great conversation. I'd just spent several weeks completing a challenging project in my writing cave, and I was truly savoring this time of refreshing calm. A young man walked by, recognized one of my friends, and stopped to chat. There was an empty chair at our table, and my friend invited Ted to sit down and visit with us. Ted had just completed a master's degree program, but this day he was dressed in the uniform of the times: shorts, ball cap, flip-flops, and a T-shirt that declared he loved a certain restaurant whose name had nothing whatsoever to do with owls.

Attractive, articulate, and clearly extroverted, Ted would have been a breath of fresh air—had it not been for his extensive use of profanity, particularly the *f* word. It was like he needed the word to inhale air and move on to his next thought. Every other word from Ted was profane, and I found myself cringing at each new onslaught. I felt as if I were being verbally slapped in the face, aurally assaulted with every sentence. After a while, turning the other cheek wasn't working, and what had been a beautiful day quickly soured into an increasingly uncomfortable situation.

I'm far from a prude, but these days very few of my friends or business associates use such off-color language. Nor do I. That had not always been the case, and I'd worked long and hard to make this change in my own life. I'm sure this made me even more sensitive to this issue.

Could I have simply allowed this young man's crude language to roll off my shoulders, realizing I would most likely never see him again? Yes. But in that instant I also realized that if I truly believed in God and trusted His Word, I had to believe He placed me in this position for a reason, and I asked myself if the reason was to learn how to keep my mouth shut or to learn how to communicate rationally and perhaps be a light in this young man's world. (Just so you know, the keeping my mouth shut option is a lesson God frequently teaches me, so I really had to pray hard about this as I sat there.)

In Dr. Laura's words, would I stand up, or would I move on?

I'll admit I'm not always good at being calm and thoughtful. Sometimes my words come out far more caustic than I intend them to. Years ago, I probably would have resorted to sarcasm. ("Do you eat with that mouth?") But on this occasion, I asked God to calm my spirit and give me words that would allow me to set a boundary that would be helpful to Ted, to me, and perhaps to the others present as well.

Feeling convicted that I needed to speak up, I took a deep breath as I said something along these lines:

"It's really nice to hear someone so passionate about life, but could I ask you a question?"

"Sure," he said with a smile.

Looking directly at him, I was careful to keep my voice calm and kind. I didn't want to sound angry or judgmental. I was about to confront him, but I didn't want this to be confrontational. *Please, Lord, give me the right words.*

"I'm wondering if you're aware how much you swear and how offensive that might be for some people? It's actually making me uncomfortable, as if I were being slapped over and over again. I've been sitting here trying to figure out whether I should say something. You seem like a smart guy, gifted and good-looking, so you obviously don't need to talk like that, and it doesn't do you justice. I'm kind of out of touch with young people today—is that generally how your friends talk? I just wondered."

Then, I did what I couldn't have done without God's help. I stopped talking and prayed that God would make Himself known.

My heart was pounding, and my friends' jaws dropped at my boldness. This could have gone any number of ways, not all of them good, but to this young man's credit, he sincerely apologized, clearly sorry that he'd offended me and put a damper on my day. This led to a wonderful conversation about words and their meanings (something very dear to me), and then we talked about effectively setting healthy boundaries verbally. We eventually got around to a spirited discussion about faith. The entire situation turned into what I call a *God-cidence* moment, and I'd like to think all of us left that day with something to ponder about God's purpose for our lives and why He places us in situations that test our mettle. And all of this happened because I spoke up and set a boundary about using profanity.

I had the choice to stand up or move on, and I chose to stand up in a way that I felt was pleasing to God. Was I afraid? Yes—but not that what I was doing was wrong. I was only afraid that I wouldn't say the right words and would miss the opportunity God had provided.

The Moment Is Now

On Palm Sunday at Harvest Church in Watauga, Texas, pastor Chuck Angel challenged those of us in the pews to find the courage to open the door to change and choice. Here are a few of the copious notes I took when I wasn't shouting "Amen!"

> When opportunity knocks, we need to have courage to over-
> come fear. There's a difference between understanding what

you should do and choosing to do it. The tipping point takes us from knowing what we ought to do to making the decision to act.

God will direct our paths, but He won't take the step for us. Some of us will stop on the journey. It's not just knowing— it's going. Often, there is a gap in the middle between knowing and going.

Life is a parade of "now" moments, not a series of tomorrows. No future moment is more significant than now.

Confronting the Difficult People in Our Lives

Those of us with difficult people in our lives need to learn to stand up and confront them (or our own issues) or to move on. We need courage to walk through doors to freedom. Simply identifying that a door exists isn't enough; we need the courage to walk through it.

Is this your "now" moment?

The SANITY Goal

For me, the journey to setting healthy boundaries has been rocky. Years ago, I'd reached the end of my rope (yet again) with my adult son, Chris, but this time something was different—this time I turned solely to my Bible, crying out to God not only for wisdom and discernment but also for clear answers to a situation that was continually breaking my heart. Chris was in jail (yet again), and for the first time I felt a powerful conviction that it was time for both of us to start a new life journey. For some reason, this time, enough really was enough, and things were going to change—I was going to change—regardless of whether Chris changed one iota.

I've always been a writer. That's what I do—it's how I most often process my life. One day, as I was reading Scripture, writing notes, and pouring my heart out on the pages, God imparted a powerful lesson to me. Personally, I learn best using visuals, acronyms, lists, bullet points, words of affirmation…tools that help me to remember important things. So on this day, in almost no time I had developed six critical actions that I knew I needed to do in my relationship with my son. As I read and reread the pages, an acronym formed, and I wrote this at the top of the page.

"Set boundaries and find SANITY."

I'm one of the most severely boundary-challenged individuals I know, so it wasn't a surprise that during this time of seeking answers, God would lay that conviction on my heart. My own boundary-setting backsliding often left tire tracks of poor choices all over my bruised heart. I knew this was a problem I struggled with.

As a sinner who is acutely aware of what it means to be in bondage, my personal goal since making my own U-turn toward God has been to do my best to live a life that is pleasing to Him and to help others find freedom from their painful pasts. The need to set healthy boundaries consistently plays an active role in many areas in my life. However, since stumbling on the Six Steps to SANITY, I've found it easier to get back on the horse when I fall off.

The Spiritual Goal

In her book *A Woman's Passionate Pursuit of God*, my friend Karol Ladd has written a wonderful study of the New Testament book of Philippians. Written by the apostle Paul while imprisoned in Rome, Philippians is actually a letter to the people of Philippi, teaching early Christians how to experience a true satisfaction of the soul. His story of resilient joy, consistent contentment, and a peace that passes all understanding is one of the most quoted stories in the Bible.

Karol begins her book by weaving together the story of Paul and Silas's journey to Philippi, recounting the way Lydia was converted, Paul cast demons out of a slave girl, and he and Silas were arrested, beaten, and thrown into a dungeon prison.

> Have you ever thought you were following God's guidance or leading and found yourself in a real mess of a situation? It can tend to make you want to doubt God and question His work in your life. Did I really follow God's direction? Does He really care about my situation? Why would God allow this

to happen to me if I am following His will? The questions are valid, but we will soon see that God often allows the difficulties in our lives for a greater purpose. He will not leave us in the midst of our troubles. The important thing is to learn to react to our situations and challenges with faith and not fear.[2]

Stories of faith-filled and seemingly fearless men and women abound throughout the Bible. Time after time, these persecuted individuals realized that their power to overcome difficulties came from God and not from themselves. They learned to react to their situations and challenges differently. They chose to look to God. Karol leads us once again to that truth.

We too can learn to turn our eyes upward and have a different response than the rest of the world when it comes to challenges in our life. We are jars of clay with a great and mighty God who is able to bring beauty out of any situation. He will give us the strength we need to endure and persevere through the not-so-perfect places in our lives.[3]

As we keep our eye on the goal to find freedom from challenging relationships with difficult people, to learn how and when to stand up or move on, let us not forget, as Karol writes, to turn our eyes upward during the journey.

Partners on the Journey

I wondered what setting boundaries with difficult people looks like from different perspectives, so more than a year ago I began to distribute a questionnaire to men and women around the country. I'll include many of the candid and helpful responses throughout the book. I have changed some of the names to honor respondents' requests for anonymity.

Also, because I'm a layman in the world of Christian counseling, I invited a professional counselor to join us from time to time, someone who is better experienced therapeutically to help us on the journey. Bernis Riley holds a bachelor of science degree in medical technology from

Sam Houston State University and a master of arts degree in counseling from Liberty University. Her major experience is in trauma-related disorders and family therapy. Bernis is a licensed professional counselor and a certified brief strategic family therapist. She is a member of the American Association of Christian Counselors and the Christian Counselors of Texas. Bernis is completing a doctoral program in psychology from California Southern University.

Bernis conducts a thriving private counseling practice called Soul-Care in the Dallas–Ft. Worth area of Texas. I asked her how she would describe her work.

> Life has a way of handing us problems that we are not prepared to handle. It's important to remember that you don't have to face those problems alone. A trusted counselor can help you find peace and hope when you are overwhelmed or confused by the problems you are facing. Counseling can help you overcome the issues you struggle with, like depression, anger, fear, and anxiety. It can also help people out of the chaos of codependency, enabling, and childhood abuse.

As we proceed on the road to setting boundaries with difficult people, Bernis will provide soul-searching questions and helpful tips in a section called "SANITY Support" at the end of each chapter. These supportive points to consider will help you apply what you have learned from each chapter to your life right now. Drawing on her experience as a Christian counselor, Bernis has also provided sample scripts and letters at the end of this book to help you approach the difficult people in your life.

Individual Choices

Learning to understand God's plan is a lifelong journey that can often take us into uncharted territory. The quest to know our purpose in life has confounded men and women since the beginning of time. Just when we think we've got things nailed down, the rug gets pulled out from under us, and we find ourselves looking at our lives from an entirely different perspective. Never is this more true than when it comes to setting healthy boundaries with difficult people in uncomfortable situations.

Some of the boundary choices we face will be life-changing. Yet the monumental choices we make that dramatically change the course of our lives are actually no more important than the individual choices we make in the everyday moments of life. Combined, they make us who we are—a rich tapestry of experience woven together by our choices.

SANITY Support

1. Purchase an inexpensive spiral notebook or steno pad that will fit in your purse or briefcase. Use it in conjunction with reading this book, starting with the questions below.

2. Who are the difficult people in your life? With whom are you hesitant to set healthy boundaries?

3. What keeps you from setting those boundaries?

4. Which growth action—standing up or moving on—are you willing to take with the difficult people in your life so that you are no longer stuck in neutral?

2

Understanding Boundaries

Seldom does a day go by that I'm not reminded of the importance of setting boundaries. Of course, I may be more acutely aware of the topic because of this book series, but that doesn't change the fact that many Christians seem to be having trouble with this aspect of life. I hear from confused and frustrated people all the time from all over the country. The entire concept of boundaries can be hard to grasp even for those of us who know we are living in the throes of boundary dysfunction.

There is no sugarcoating this truth. Without necessary boundaries, our lives become unmanageable. Period. But how do we know if poor boundaries are the problem?

Think of it this way. Let's say we get into our car, turn the key, and nothing happens. There are only so many things that could be wrong. Are we out of fuel? If not, the next thing to check is the battery, then the alternator, then the carburetor, and so on. Addressing the possibilities one by one in a logical order is the best way to diagnose and fix the problem. Eventually, you (or a talented mechanic) will find the root of the problem. But think about it—if your car doesn't start, the first thing you address probably won't be the air in your tires.

It's much the same in diagnosing what's wrong in our challenging relationships with difficult people. There's a "first things first" list to review, and at the top of that list is this: Check personal boundaries.

Our Responsibility

A successful relationship is comprised of two individuals who each has a clearly defined sense of his or her own identity and personal boundaries. It's our responsibility (and no one else's) to understand our identity and define our personal boundaries, to identify where we start and end and where the other person starts. Just as a property owner may be angry when someone trespasses on his land, so too we become angry and hurt when other people trespass our personal boundaries.

Yet if we don't know what those boundaries are, how can we enforce our own or respect others'? Unclear boundaries can be one reason we have very destructive and dysfunctional relationships. On the other hand, depression, codependency, anxiety, and many other conditions can improve by becoming aware of and enforcing our personal boundaries.

For the past several years, I've had a desire to help laypeople like me get a handle on what interpersonal boundaries are, how they work, and how to improve our interaction with others. There are a great many books available on the topic from trained professionals, and I quote some of them in this book. However, trained professionals often resort to technical, clinical terms, such as *enmeshment, triangulation, disassociation, subjugation, excessive detachment, victimhood* or *martyrdom*, and of course the catchall, *codependency*.

But I'm not going to do that. You won't need an advanced psychology degree to comprehend my theory or method. My advice for dealing with difficult people is based on experience and translating some of that clinical language the professionals use into everyday, understandable English.

Understanding what a boundary is and is not is critical if we're to achieve our goal of finding freedom from challenging relationships. Being able to wrap our brains around the foundational principles of boundaries is an important first step on our road to finding SANITY.

Those of us raised in dysfunctional families have probably had little experience with healthy boundaries. A lack of proper boundaries is often at the root of dysfunction. Therefore, learning how to understand

and establish boundaries must be an important goal in our personal growth. In order to achieve this, however, we must overcome things like low self-esteem and passivity. We must learn to identify and respect our rights and needs and become skilled at assertively taking care of ourselves in relationships. This process allows our true selves to emerge, and suddenly healthy boundaries become the fences that provide us with safety—something we may never have experienced in childhood.

There are a great many reasons why we may have allowed some of our relationships to grow into things that choke the very life out of us. I will do my best to address key topics, but it's impossible to cover all of the varied nuances of why we do the things we do, and I encourage you to seek out a professional Christian counselor if addressing this issue appears to be more than you can handle on your own.

In the meantime, keep reading.

What Is a Boundary?

Webster's defines a boundary as "something that marks or fixes a limit…a territory, border, frontier."

The most easily recognizable boundaries are property lines. You've probably seen No Trespassing signs posted on private property. These signs send a clear message: If you cross the line you will be prosecuted! This type of physical boundary is easy to picture and understand because it's tangible; you can actually see and touch the sign. On the other hand, personal boundaries are harder to define because the lines are invisible. Also, they can change and are unique to each individual.

If you're struggling with difficult people, the problem probably has to do with absent, misdrawn, or poorly defined boundaries—yours or theirs.

Why We Need Boundaries

On our journey to make healthy choices that will change our lives, one of the first things we must learn is why we need boundaries in the first place.

Quite simply, we need them because God has mandated them. This is the way He wants us to live. God set the first boundary in the Garden of Eden.

> The LORD God took the man and put him in the Garden of Eden to work it and take care of it. And the LORD God commanded the man, "You are free to eat from any tree in the garden; but you must not eat from the tree of the knowledge of good and evil, for when you eat from it you will certainly die" (Genesis 2:15-17).

As we know, Adam and Eve overstepped this boundary, and that created catastrophic consequences.

The most basic boundary-setting word is *no*. ("No, I can't babysit tonight. I love my grandkids, but you can't drop them off at my house without asking first.") It lets others know that you exist apart from them and that you are in control of you. Being clear about your yes and your no is a theme that runs throughout the Bible. Being clear about the consequences when you set a boundary is also critical.

> All you need to say is simply "Yes" or "No"; anything beyond this comes from the evil one (Matthew 5:37).

> Above all, my brothers and sisters, do not swear—not by heaven or by earth or by anything else. All you need to say is a simple "Yes" or "No." Otherwise you will be condemned (James 5:12).

Boundaries and Selfishness

Unfortunately, people often view boundaries negatively, as if setting boundaries were just an excuse to reject others or be selfish.

Nothing could be further from the truth, as Drs. Henry Cloud and John Townsend share in their seminal book *Boundaries: When to Say Yes, When to Say No to Take Control of Your Life*. In my own journey of trying to better understand the reasons I had difficulty setting healthy boundaries, this pivotal book gave me biblical insight into the world of intangible boundaries—the boundaries that define who we are at the core of our being.

This is the benchmark resource for Christians who desire to gain insight and wisdom about a subject that is far more common than we might imagine—the destructive patterns that keep people dysfunctional—and what God's Word really says about this. I'll refer often to this book and to the wisdom of its authors. These words especially spoke to me:

> For years, Christians have been taught that protecting their spiritual and emotional property is selfish. Yet God is interested in people loving others, and you can't love others unless you have received love inside yourself…

> This principle is illustrated when Solomon says, "Above all else, guard your heart, for it is the wellspring of life" (Proverbs 4:23). When we "watch over" our hearts (the home of our treasures), we guard them.[1]

Boundaries and Emotional Choices

Another reason we have trouble setting boundaries, and one of the most prevalent, is that we're too emotionally involved in situations to consider them objectively. In such cases, we often rely on our feelings rather than thinking the matter through. When possible, we should make choices calmly, rationally, and with prayerful wisdom, especially when they significantly affect our relationships. Unfortunately, when communicating with difficult people who get under our skin, many of us often react emotionally. If we truly want freedom in challenging relationships, we're going to have to do some deep soul-searching work regarding our emotions and how to better control them.

When it comes to emotions, many of us are like gerbils on a wheel going round and round, seemingly unable to stop the out-of-control habits we've developed. We do this because…

- We think we don't have a choice.
- We've neglected to define our personal boundaries.
- Our own destructive patterns get in the way.
- We've lost sight of our priorities.

- We don't understand our identity—our place within the family of God.

In short, the problem isn't that we have difficult people in our lives, but that we respond to them inappropriately, almost always because they push our emotional buttons.

The Freedom of Boundaries

Knowing what a boundary is and is not may seem like basic information, but it's important that we change the old recordings that still live inside our brains, telling us lies about boundaries that Satan has successfully used to keep us in bondage.

A boundary is...	A boundary is not...
healthy	rejection
necessary	selfish
biblical	sinful
respectful	disrespectful
loving	dishonoring

Personal Boundaries

Personal boundaries are limits or borders that define where you end and others begin. Your personal boundaries are defined by the amount of physical and emotional space you allow between yourself and others. Personal boundaries also help you decide what types of communication, behavior, and interaction you accept from others. The boundaries you set define whether you have healthy or unhealthy relationships. I like the way Henry Cloud and John Townsend clarify this.

> Any confusion of responsibility and ownership in our lives is a problem of boundaries. Just as homeowners set physical property lines around their land, we need to set mental, physical, emotional, and spiritual boundaries around our heart, to help us distinguish what is our responsibility and what isn't. The

inability to set appropriate boundaries at appropriate times with the appropriate people can be very destructive. And this is one of the most serious problems facing Christians today. Many sincere, dedicated believers struggle with tremendous confusion about when it is biblically appropriate to set limits.[2]

Personal property lines define who we are and influence all areas of our lives. Most of us are so concerned about our challenging circumstances, we don't realize that intangible boundaries define many other facets of our daily lives as well. We need to recognize that we have boundaries in many areas, including these:

- physical boundaries
- psychological boundaries (also known as emotional and intellectual boundaries)
- financial boundaries
- spiritual boundaries

The two main types of boundaries we're most familiar with are physical and psychological.

Physical Boundaries

Physical boundaries define and protect your body, your personal space, and your sense of privacy. Other physical boundaries involve clothes, shelter, safety, money, space, noise, and so on.

Your physical boundaries need to be strong to protect you from harm. If you have a deep wound that goes untreated, you expose yourself to infection, which can result in serious, life-threatening consequences. Protecting your physical boundaries is essential for your health and well-being.

Have you ever tried to have a conversation with someone who stood too close to you? Your immediate and automatic reaction is to take a step back in order to reset your personal space. By doing this you send a nonverbal message that when people stand so close, you feel an invasion of your personal space. If the person continues to move closer, your next step might be to verbally protect your boundary by telling him or her to stop crowding you. Again you are protecting your personal space by setting your boundary.

Here are a few additional examples of physical boundary invasions:

- inappropriate touching, such as making unwanted sexual advances

- physical abuse, such as pushing, shoving, or slapping

- looking through others' personal documents and belongings

- not respecting others' personal space, such as barging into your boss's office without knocking

As someone who has survived early childhood abuse and extreme domestic violence, I've become acutely aware of protecting my physical boundaries. Yet it took years of poor choices and painful experiences to understand how those violated boundaries affected virtually every aspect of my life decades later.

Psychological Boundaries

Just as physical boundaries define who can touch us, how someone can touch us, and how physically close another may approach us, psychological boundaries define where our feelings end and another's begins. Many of us have no understanding of this differentiation.

Psychological boundaries comprise the thinking part of who we are—what we put into our heads and goes on inside there. This part of us is what we carry in our minds: our knowledge, wisdom, experience, memories, reflections, speculations, vocabulary, opinions, and in some cases, the lies we've believed. It includes our emotions and thoughts, our will, intellect, mind, worldview, and pattern of thinking.

Psychological boundaries are important. They protect our sense of self-esteem and our ability to separate our feelings from the feelings of others. For example, do we take responsibility for our feelings and needs and allow others to do the same? Or do we feel overly responsible for other people's feelings and needs and neglect our own? Are we able to say no? Can we ask for what we need? Are we compulsive people pleasers? Do we become upset simply because others around us are upset? Do we mimic the opinions of the people around us? The answers to these questions help us assess the strength of our psychological boundaries.

Having weak emotional boundaries is like getting caught in a hurricane with no protection. We are subject to and controlled by other people's feelings, and we can end up feeling bruised and battered.

Together, our physical and psychological boundaries define how we interact with others and allow them to interact with us. Without boundaries, others could touch us in any way they wanted, do whatever they wished with our possessions, and treat us in any way they desired. In addition, we would believe everyone else's bad behaviors are our fault, take on everyone else's problems as our own, and feel as if we have no claim to any rights. In short, our lives would be chaotic and out of our control.

Boundaries Can Be Too Rigid or Too Loose

Those whose boundaries are too rigid shut everyone out of their lives. They appear aloof and distant and won't talk about feelings or show emotions. They exhibit extreme self-sufficiency and don't ask for help when they honestly need it. They don't allow anyone to get physically or emotionally close. They might as well live in a house surrounded by an immense wall with no gates. No one is allowed in.

On the other hand, those whose boundaries are too loose put their hands on strangers and let others touch them inappropriately. They may be sexually promiscuous, confuse sex and love, be driven to be in a sexual relationship, and get too close to others too fast. They may take on other people's feelings as their own, easily become emotionally overwhelmed, give too much, take too much, and be in constant need of reassurance. They may expect others to read their minds, think they can read other people's minds, say yes when they want to say no, and feel responsible for other people's feelings. Those with loose boundaries often lead chaotic lives, full of drama, as if they lived in houses with no fences, gates, locks, or even doors.

I'll be honest with you—I've experienced both sides of this coin. Before I became a Christian, I had one long-term boyfriend after another who quickly turned into one fiancé after another, always moving into my place while we planned weddings that never occurred. My life as a New Age secular humanist was a constant search for someone or something to fill the aching hole in my spirit and soul. I often say I was so open-minded that my brain slipped out. Back then, my boundaries were far too loose.

When I became a follower of Christ, the pendulum swung in the opposite direction, and that was equally destructive. As I began to see the mistakes I had made in my earlier life, I put up more and more walls and instilled increasingly rigid boundaries to protect myself from making the same mistakes. The more aware I became of God's plan for my life, the more I understood how Satan was working feverishly in my spirit to construct roadblocks and detours at every junction. Setting boundaries that were too rigid kept me safe—but isolated. Finding a healthy middle ground, or balance, has been an ongoing journey. It still is.

Violated Boundaries

All healthy relationships have limits on what is appropriate. If a boss is demanding more of you than he should, or if you are feeling victimized in your own marriage, you are experiencing a boundary violation, and that's a serious matter. Many children who have suffered verbal, physical, emotional, or sexual abuse grow up with no concept of how to set healthy boundaries. They know walls, cell bars, and hiding places, but not boundaries. One of the aftereffects of child abuse is the inability to construct or enforce personal boundaries. However, this aftereffect holds true at any age—when someone violates our boundaries, we can have a devastatingly difficult time setting healthy boundaries as life goes on.

Do you know when someone is violating your space—your personal boundaries?

We are making progress on our journey to freedom when we recognize boundary violations and are strong enough to let people know when they are crossing the line. In times like these, we can say, "If you violate my property, then I will…" or "This is my territory, and you may not enter without my permission."

The Weight of Boundaries

Another particular boundary has greatly affected my life and the lives of literally millions of people. The next book in this series will focus solely on this area, but I felt compelled to mention it here as well.

The obesity epidemic affects an estimated 72 million people in America—roughly 34 percent of our population. This figure doesn't take into consideration those who are simply overweight, which is different from being obese.

I've struggled with severely fluctuating weight issues since I ran away from home as a teen to marry a man whose extreme physical abuse almost killed me. At 16, when I was literally running for my life and pregnant, I tried to protect myself by building a boundary of excess weight. My scale once hit 300 pounds.

When I had gastric bypass weight loss surgery in October of 2000, I weighed 280 pounds. I've managed to keep off the 120 pounds I lost in the year after surgery, but I'm keenly aware that obesity quite often stems from violated boundaries.

Anne Katherine is a psychotherapist, a licensed mental-health counselor, and a popular author known for her pioneering work in developing effective programs for recovery from food addiction and discovery of life purpose. In her book *Boundaries: Where You End and I Begin,* she includes a special letter to overeaters that I found particularly powerful.

> If you are carrying extra weight, it may be providing you with a boundary as well. Weight is a good way to keep people at a distance when people have taken too much from you. It literally extends your physical boundary.

If you were abused as a child, fat can feel like a comforting shield. It is a physical barricade against people who might harm you.

Food and fat seem to protect us. Perhaps you eat more when you feel threatened. Perhaps you eat when you know someone is going to take more from you than you want to give. Perhaps you eat when you're with a person who assaults your boundaries.

Boundary development is an important companion to an eating recovery program. Not until you know you can protect yourself from intrusion and theft will you be safe without the extra weight.[3]

I'll address this epidemic issue in *Setting Boundaries with Food*, and I'll show how the Six Steps to SANITY can help free us from the pounds that weigh down our bodies, souls, and spirits. Please visit my website, AllisonBottke.com, to find out more about this upcoming book.

How Do We Know?

Do you wonder how to know whether your boundaries are healthy? If you can answer yes to one or more of the questions below, you may need to assess your personal property lines and start making different choices about those boundaries.

- Do some people take advantage of you?
- Do you sometimes have trouble saying no?
- Do you often suffer from feelings of guilt?
- Do you ever feel as though you have no control over some areas of your life?
- Do you try to have too much control over some areas of your life?
- Do you avoid conversations you know you should have?

- Do you wish you could be more assertive and in control?

- Do you lose patience with certain people or personality types?

- Do you feel anxious before a difficult conversation?

- Do you think of what you should have said after a conversation is over?

- Do you know when someone is violating your space?

Now That We Understand Boundary Basics

The journey to find SANITY doesn't happen overnight. It isn't just a matter of understanding what the word means or what types of boundaries exist, although these are important things to know. Understanding boundaries really begins when we stop seeing ourselves as helpless in a drowning situation and realize how much power we have over our actions and emotions. More important, understanding boundaries is also being aware of what God's Word teaches us about the critical aspect of protecting our hearts. One of the most powerful actions we can take in life is to choose to be in relationships that bring out the best in us—that nurture our heart—and that allow us to bring out the best in others as well.

SANITY Support

1. Take time to examine your relationships by answering the "How Do We Know" questions above.

2. Which of your relationships lack healthy boundaries?

3. What types of boundaries have been violated in those relationships? Physical? Emotional? Mental? Psychological? Spiritual?

3

Embracing the Most Important Relationship

If we believe wholeheartedly that God is personally involved in our lives, we would expect that He has something specific in mind for us to do while we're here on earth.

In their book *Being Christian: Exploring Where You, God, and Life Connect*, authors Stephen Arterburn and John Shore address four things every Christian will need at some point in life: answers, guidance, confirmation, and inspiration. They address a question that has laid heavy on the heart of many believers: Does God have a plan for me?

> He certainly does. God's plan is for you to accept the fact that He loves you, has always loved you, and will always love you. God's plan for you is to trust in the truth of who He is, and in what He has done for you. It's for you to open yourself up to the wondrous powers of the Holy Spirit within you. God's Big Plan is for everyone who believes in Him to be gathered around Him after they've departed from this veil of tears, and to spend eternity in the utter delight and fulfillment of His incomparable presence.
>
> In a nutshell, God's plan for you is to love Him, and to then use that love to serve Him and others.
>
> In addition to serving God and loving others, there's something else in God's plan. It's a huge part of why He created us,

and why He sticks with us even when we mess up. It's called relationship.[1]

In other words, we matter to God. But how much does God matter to us?

During the years before I wrote *Setting Boundaries with Your Adult Children*, a disproportionate amount of my time was spent caught up in the drama, chaos, and crisis that characterized the world of my drug-addicted adult son. His life was made up of one poor choice after another. Unfortunately, as a classic codependent with extreme enabling tendencies, I often responded in ways that contributed to the painful dynamic. Year after year, decade after decade, our increasingly dysfunctional relationship often took precedence over everything else in my life.

I'm not alone in this journey. It's easy to become consumed in the drama and negativity that surrounds some of our more difficult interpersonal relationships.

A Life-Changing Truth

One of Satan's most insidious strategies to attack and influence the children of God has been to keep them too involved with challenging relationships to care about a relationship with the One who cares the most—Jesus Christ.

And time is running out.

Recently, I had the opportunity to hear Kay Arthur speak at the annual Christian Women in Media Association conference in Nashville. As always, Kay spoke with great passion, purpose, and wisdom.

> What does it mean to be living "for such a time as this"? Ladies, if we are here for such a time as this, we must understand what time it is! We need to know what's going on in our world— and what's going on isn't pretty! We need mighty men and women of valor who are trained for war, and the sword of the Spirit is the Word of God. This is our weapon, and we must learn to use it. Our world is caroming out of control, and the foundation of ministry—any ministry—has to be what *God*

says—not what *we* think. And the only way to know what God says is by reading His Word.

As I've talked with hundreds of women and men around the world about the topic of setting healthy boundaries, I'm convinced we have a crippling epidemic that must be addressed. Quite simply, our relationships are out of kilter. We're confused about what is and isn't our responsibility, and we're responding in overly emotional ways that do not honor God or our relationship with His Son. We've lost sight of God's priorities and purpose. However, as Kay said, it's not about what *I* think; it's about what *God* says. And when it comes to priorities, God has some very clear standards for how He wants us to live.

> Jesus replied: "'Love the Lord your God with all your heart and with all your soul and with all your mind.' This is the first and greatest commandment. And the second is like it: 'Love your neighbor as yourself.' All the Law and the Prophets hang on these two commandments" (Matthew 22:37-40).

Clearly, God wants us to be in loving relationships, starting with Himself. Yet relationships are being destroyed, hearts broken, and families fractured as good Christian men and women forget what God has said about the most important priorities in life—to love Him first and to love our neighbors. This is the very essence of the gospel message.

In his landmark book *The Hole in Our Gospel*, Richard Stearns talks transparently about the struggles he has had as a Christian, particularly with respect to the implications of the gospel of Jesus Christ.

> In the end, responding to the gospel is not something meant for nations or communities or even churches; it is meant for individuals—one person at a time. The three greatest commandments—to love God, love our neighbors, and make disciples in all nations—are the work of God's people, those who have first responded to the good news themselves. It takes transformed people to transform the world. But each of us must first have our own "Damascus Road" experience, our "Thomas moment," in which our doubts fall away and we drop

to our knees and acknowledge our Lord and our God (see
Acts 22:1-11 and John 20:24-28). Only then does the journey
of faith truly begin.[2]

We can talk about setting healthy boundaries until the cows come
home, but without the foundation of faith, it's ultimately a moot point.
Faith requires a response to God's commandments, and God's most
important commandment is that we love Him—that we have a relationship with Him.

Step One: Love the Lord Your God

It starts by acknowledging Jesus Christ as our Savior—our Lord.

Ryan Northcutt is the pastor of a small but rapidly growing community church in Haltom City, Texas. He is a man of God who truly understands how to acknowledge and love Jesus, and this is the first church
he and his lovely wife, Annie, have pastored. In a powerful message
focused on relationship as opposed to religion, Pastor Ryan talked pas-
sionately about a personal God who understands what it's like to live in
this world—to be involved with people, challenges, troubles, and trials.

> We can't do it on our own. When we trust in ourselves, it's
> too hard. If we rely on only ourselves, we will be left wanting.
>
> When we are separated from God, we feel it—we may not
> know what is missing from our life, but we know something
> is. When that something becomes a relationship with the Lord,
> it's impossible to live the same way. When our relationship
> with the Lord grows, we grow.
>
> It's not about what *we* have to do to get to God, for by grace
> we are all saved. It's about what *Jesus* did for us to get to us.
>
> There is one way to have a relationship with God. It's not
> complicated, but it is profound. It's found in Romans 10:9-
> 10, where it is written, "If you declare with your mouth, 'Jesus
> is Lord,' and believe in your heart that God raised him from
> the dead, you will be saved. For it is with your heart that you
> believe and are justified, and it is with your mouth that you
> profess your faith and are saved" (Romans 10:9-10).

Christians need to focus not only on *getting* saved but also on *living* saved. Not only on *receiving* grace but also on *walking* in grace. The spiritual fruit produced through this relationship is not a requisite to keep salvation, but rather is the natural harvest of a truly changed heart. It is impossible to plant an apple seed and not in due time see the return of an apple tree. In the same way it is impossible for the person who has received the seed of the gospel by way of salvation not to see the return of a spiritual life that is dedicated to growing that which was planted. When we understand this deeply satisfying gift it will permeate everything we do in life.

God used His servant Pastor Ryan to impart this powerful truth to everyone who sat in the packed church that Sunday. Those whose hearts were open to willingly hear the message could not help but leave changed. This is how the Spirit of God works. But He can't do this work if we don't have a relationship with Him. This begins when we acknowledge Him.

Step Two: Love Your Neighbor as Yourself

In America, the land of electric garage-door openers and overly busy lives, many people rarely see their neighbors. Even worse, people often think of their neighbors as nuisances with barking dogs, noisy children, and overhanging tree branches. How can we possibly love those around us? For some, "Love your neighbor" has become little more than a cliché. What does it really mean for us in twenty-first-century America?

Needing answers, I did what any self-respecting woman of the times would do when faced with a serious question. I went online and googled it.

As I read one inductive Bible study after another and the Scripture passages they referenced, I felt the Spirit of the Lord open my eyes to another important aspect of setting boundaries with difficult people.

God calls us to love our neighbors, regardless of how difficult they might be. He doesn't say, "Love your neighbor when everything is peachy keen and rosy." He calls us to love them—period. In some instances, this will require intentional discipline. This is something He wants us to *do*, trusting that in the doing, we become who He wants us to be.

What are we becoming as children of God? What life-changing lessons are we learning as we grow? Do the difficult people in our lives have anything to do with God's bigger picture for us? How can we set healthy boundaries and still treat these difficult people with love, like a neighbor, as God commands?

Here's one of the many studies I found on the meaning of "love your neighbor." It's from AllAboutGod.com.

Love Thy Neighbor—Christ's Answer to Religion

Love thy neighbor was, in part, Jesus' answer when the Pharisees, the chief religious sect of that day, asked Him about the greatest commandment in the Law (see Matthew 22:36-40). These religious leaders had made almost an art form of classifying all the various laws and giving them relative degrees of importance, so in asking Jesus this question, their aim was to test Him. His answer stunned them: "'Love the Lord your God with all your heart and with all your soul and with all your mind.' This is the first and greatest commandment. And the second is like it: 'Love your neighbor as yourself.' All the Law and the Prophets hang on these two commandments."

Jesus was summing up all the law in these two statements. If we love the Lord God with all our heart, soul and mind, loving our neighbor is the natural result. The question then is, who is our neighbor, and how do we love him or her?

Let's look at who Jesus says our neighbor is: "You have heard that it was said, 'Love your neighbor and hate your enemy.' But I tell you: Love your enemies and pray for those who persecute you" (Matthew 5:43).

Is our neighbor more than the guy next door? Could he or she be someone in our community or almost anyone we meet?

Could our enemies also be our neighbors? Jesus says that it's so. But how can we love someone who acts hatefully toward us?

When we love God with all our heart, soul, mind and strength, we grow to recognize that everyone is part of His creation. Will everyone be in heaven? No, but that's not because God doesn't desire that to be the case. His Word tells us that God desires that all would be saved (1 Timothy 2:4). So it's clear that God sees all of us as potential children. Because He lives outside of time and has seen the end from the beginning, He also knows who will choose salvation and who will not. For us, that is where faith comes in. It is not for us to know who will choose Him and who will not, but we are called to be His witnesses. In order to fulfill that calling, we must love others enough to desire their salvation just as He does.

Here's the good news for those who find this teaching difficult: Nowhere does it say we have to like our neighbor![3]

Love Your Neighbor—Get to Know Jesus

Loving our neighbors means respecting others and regarding their needs and desires as highly as we regard our own. Keeping this commandment, however, is likely to require the supernatural assistance only God, through Christ, can provide.

How can we learn to love the guy next door with the barking dog, especially when we don't even like him? Perhaps the secret is to recognize that our neighbor, whether it's the guy next door, the checker at the local grocery store, the Sunday school teacher at church, or perhaps even our spouse, ex-spouse, or sibling, is someone as worthy of God's love as you and I are.

Could it be that the way we begin to love our neighbor is to get to know Christ, the living Word of God? It's human nature to emulate those we admire most, so in getting to know Christ, we'll discover a God worthy of our wholehearted love, and perhaps our neighbor will see that love in us.

When we embrace the most important relationship, perhaps every other relationship to follow will be changed as a result.

Author, speaker, and dear friend Eva Marie Everson learned to set boundaries with a loved one who balances precariously on a high wire of mental illness. Here is a sample of what she has discovered.

> As Christians, we often forget to draw boundary lines, thinking that loving our neighbor means allowing someone to crucify us as they did Christ. When Jesus told us to turn the other cheek, I don't believe this is what he meant. This is not helpful to someone who doesn't know acceptable or healthy boundaries; it perpetuates the problem and causes rifts between brothers and sisters. I have had to learn to say, "I love you, but I cannot let you speak to me…treat me…talk to me…in this manner." I extend love and grace but do not allow abuse.

A Fact of Life

There will always be difficult people to deal with in our lives here on earth. We will face difficult situations and circumstances as well. Unexpected things happen, and we're sometimes unprepared, blindsided.

For example, not too long ago I experienced a betrayal that sent me into a tailspin. I could never have prepared for this. I had depended for years on the love, loyalty, and support of this family member. We live in different states, so I called, wrote letters, and sent e-mail and text messages. I prayed for her, for us. As the situations leading up to the betrayal intensified, I ran the gamut of emotional responses. I begged, bargained, argued, apologized, blamed, threatened, and justified. Our conversations ranged from calm and rational to explosive and emotional. I cried out to God for wisdom and discernment as month after month our communication spiraled downward.

For almost two years I lived on the gerbil's wheel of dysfunction, going around and around with this person but never resolving anything. But finally, one day I reached the place where I had to say, "Enough is enough. This is not how God wants me to live, and I can't do this anymore."

I had to establish a firm boundary—one that has had significant consequences.

To be truly healthy, we must be able to let go of perceived insults, injustices, and disappointments. And sometimes, severing all contact with someone (for a season or for a lifetime) is the only way you can begin to heal. In my case, the decision to sever this relationship for a season was the culmination of years of disharmony and dysfunction. I would no longer accept the tirade of accusations that everything in the current situation was my fault. The time had come for me to stop taking the blame for years of increasingly toxic interactions.

Sometimes the roles we play in our families reenact long-standing scripts and dramas. Such was the case in this instance. After a long history of difficulty resolving our problems with each other, we had reached a place where toxic feelings like jealousy, resentment, and contempt raged. No relationship is black-and-white; seldom is one person to blame when communication breaks down in a relationship. Yet my truth was decidedly different from the truth this family member clung to and hurled at me like a dagger.

As Eva Marie said earlier, we can extend love and grace and at the same time not allow someone to mistreat us.

I've learned a great deal as a result of this painful situation, and through it all my relationship with the Lord has grown deeper. Often, when we're caught up in challenging relationships with difficult people, we don't realize how they may have weakened our relationship with God, reducing the quantity and quality of our time with the Lord and our intimacy with Him. God continues to teach me new relationship lessons in my daily walk with Him.

I've been deeply wounded in this family relationship, and I'm not sure what the future holds. However, I trust that God will bring something good out of the pain.

> Forget the former things; do not dwell on the past. See, I am doing a new thing! Now it springs up; do you not perceive it? I am making a way in the wilderness and streams in the wasteland (Isaiah 43:18-19).

My prayer is that you have not hit such a point of desperation in your relationship with a difficult person. But if you have, rest assured that you can find freedom from all bondage at the foot of the cross, where you can find a relationship that will never betray or fail you. From this place of love and healing you can begin to restore what you have lost.

How Do We Do It?

Ultimately, the spirit of reconciliation will always reflect the heart of God.

The Six Steps to SANITY can guide us on our journey as we learn how to respond to the difficult people in our lives. But first we must be aware of and nurture the most vital relationship—our relationship with the Most High God. How do we tangibly demonstrate that we have been transformed by God? How can our lives be characterized by such authentic signs as compassion, mercy, justice, and love?

Quite simply, we cannot do this on our own—our sinful nature will keep us from extending love and grace. Only through God's help can we receive a new nature.

If we are pieces in God's great jigsaw puzzle, and if no single piece is insignificant, then the difficult people in our lives mean as much to God as we do. This can sometimes be hard for us to grasp—but grasp it we must.

SANITY Support

1. How do you define love? In other words, how do you know if you are loved?

2. What would a loving relationship between you and the difficult person in your life look like?

3. Do you believe that you can have strong, firm, healthy, boundaries and still love your neighbor as yourself? Why or why not?

4

Identifying Core Challenges

We need courage in order to change the way we respond to the difficult people in our lives. Sometimes finding the courage to change means understanding why we do what we do. So many components contribute to who we are today. The sad truth is, many of us have been wrapped up in pleasing others, reacting to situations, and propelling the gerbil wheel, so we've neglected to consider what may have caused the problem in the first place.

If indeed something is wrong, what exactly does "wrong" look like? What's really going on that needs to change? For many of us, answering that question will be a critical component in finding SANITY. However, reaching a place where setting healthy boundaries becomes second nature and difficult people can no longer control us isn't something that happens overnight. It's a process that requires commitment and hard work on our part. Instantaneous breakthroughs seldom happen as a result of reading one book or attending one counseling session.

But that's not to say miracles don't happen—especially as we begin to identify the core challenges and apply the Six Steps to SANITY. Personally, I can attest to several miracle moments when the Holy Spirit opened my eyes and newfound enlightenment bathed a formerly dark road with brilliant clarity. It can and does happen.

Where It Begins

For those of us who are boundary challenged, understanding what is our responsibility can sometimes be confusing. Often, we're so caught up in the drama, chaos, and crisis that unclear or violated boundaries can bring to a relationship that we neglect the very heart and center of who we are. Remember the powerful truth from Scripture we discussed in chapter 2: "Above all else, guard your heart, for everything you do flows from it" (Proverbs 4:23).

In this verse, God is telling us to protect ourselves—above all else, to put a boundary around our hearts. Not a wall that keeps others out, but a protective boundary that guards the very place where God lives, allowing everything we do to flow from it.

Life will never be pain free, and the call to guard our hearts should not be misconstrued as a way to justify selfishness. The true meaning is to guard our hearts against the deception of the world, the lies of the enemy, and the desires of the flesh so that whatever flows out of our hearts and into the lives of others comes from a desire to see ourselves and others in right relationship to God.

A Strong Heart

As we grow closer to the Lord, developing right relationships with Him and with others as well, each of us will become a positive, influencing force. Make no mistake—there is an evil one who will take notice of the change. We're not only struggling with difficult people but also fighting a daily spiritual battle. We are the targets of the enemy, and when he hurts us, it affects the people around us. This is exactly what he wants.

Satan will attack the way we think and how we feel. He will give us perplexing situations (and perplexing people) to weigh us down.

Who Are Difficult People?

There's an old saying, "One man's trash is another man's treasure." Please understand that by no means am I equating relationships to trash. I mean only that one global description for what constitutes a difficult person doesn't exist. What could be difficult to one person could be quite acceptable to another. Respondents to my questionnaire wrote that difficult people are those who...

- create problems for others
- are not willing to listen
- gossip and spread rumors
- discourage and criticize others' work to boost their own egos
- rarely cooperate
- always find something negative in someone or something

A list defining difficult people could be endless. It can go on and on, depending on your definition of a difficult person. But speaking broadly, a difficult person is someone who isn't easy to be with, someone who creates problematic situations and causes unpleasant feelings in others.

Understanding the Situation

Never forget that the enemy confounds us with difficult people and the problems they can bring. How serious is the situation? John Townsend helps us make an assessment.

> The point here is for you to understand the range of your problem clearly. Scrutinize yourself about this too. I know some people who see every relational misdemeanor as a felony, and they drive friends away. They treat someone who is five minutes late the same way they treat someone who breaks into convenience stores. Be honest about severity: mildly irritating, causing intimacy and love disruptions, creating family chaos, or causing damage or danger. This will help you to be ready for your action steps.[1]

We'll be talking about specific SANITY action steps in part 2, but in the meantime, let's look at four core challenges using the acronym RAIN:

- **R**ecognize your contribution.

- **A**ddress your personal issues.

- **I**dentify the specific problems.

- **N**ame the difficult people.

It rained earlier this morning, not long before I awoke. I began my day by opening the kitchen window and enjoying the unmistakable fragrance of fresh moisture on the ground. On this beautiful April-in-Texas morning, the birds were singing and a cool breeze was blowing. The grass and leaves glistened with the fresh rejuvenation the rain had delivered.

When our hearts weigh heavy with the burden of relationships that for whatever reason just aren't right, we can sometimes feel as though vital energy has been leeched from our very souls, leaving our hearts parched and dry. We long for a breath of fresh air and revitalizing rain.

As we enter this new season in life and determine to bring order to challenging relationships, the healing power of RAIN can bring clarity to our lives.

Recognize Your Contribution

The first step in solving any problem is to accurately identify it.

I've had the opportunity to travel the country and speak one-on-one with countless people since my first Setting Boundaries book released, and I've found that a great many of us are confused about what is and what is not our responsibility concerning the people in our lives—difficult or not. This alone can be problematic. In many cases, we've unknowingly contributed to the problems, and we need to recognize where that may be the case.

Anyone can be a difficult person to someone else. We may not want to admit it, but at one time or another, all of us have been difficult people. It's vital to determine whether you are in a situation with a difficult person or you yourself are beginning to be the difficult person.

Most of the time, difficult people do not realize they are difficult.

They don't see that they are demanding too much from other people. They think their attitude is normal.

Do you struggle with enabling, codependency, or low self-esteem? Do you need to please others or win their approval? Do you have a history of abuse? Pray that God will show you areas where you need to recognize your contribution to relational struggles and respond differently.

Address Your Personal Issues

There are a host of therapeutic terms that describe the way we behave or react and why. As I've said, it would be impossible to list all of the variations here. Besides, we are all uniquely created by God's hand, so it would be folly to suggest that we can or should squeeze ourselves into certain categories just because we're having trouble setting boundaries with difficult people. I'm not suggesting we are all in need of extensive therapy or intervention. Yet I would be remiss if I didn't include a sampling of the issues that tend to be prevalent in those of us who have difficulty setting boundaries with challenging people.

- enabling
- low self-esteem
- codependency
- the need to please
- the need for approval
- past history of abuse

Bernis Riley addresses this topic of personal issues:

> When legitimate needs for love, approval, acceptance, belonging, and so on are not met in healthy ways, personal issues develop. These personal issues can interfere with the ability to set healthy boundaries. For example, the need for approval is a God-given need. It is legitimate. However, if we go about meeting this need by not openly disagreeing, by not saying no, or by going along to get along, then we will struggle to set or

enforce healthy boundaries. The motivation for our behavior at this point in the relationship is not one of love nor is it godly; it is nothing short of a selfish attempt on our part to manage the other person's opinion about us.

The Enabling Epidemic

Countless parents and grandparents have found SANITY and sudden clarity in challenging relationships with their adult children. I've received hundreds of e-mail messages and letters from readers, many citing that their personal transformation took a big jump forward after reading a definition included very early in the book *Setting Boundaries with Your Adult Children*.

What Is the Difference Between Helping and Enabling?

Helping is doing something for someone that he is not capable of doing himself.

Enabling is doing for someone what he could and should be doing himself.

An enabler is a person who recognizes that a negative circumstance is occurring on a regular basis and yet continues to enable the person with the problem to persist with his detrimental behaviors. Simply, *enabling creates an atmosphere in which our adult children can comfortably continue their unacceptable behavior.*

When we continue to allow these behaviors, we are setting up a pattern with our children that will be hard to change. We're *enabling* their repeated inappropriate behavior. Then when we repeat the enabling pattern year after year—accepting what should be unacceptable behavior and instilling bad habits—it eventually becomes as natural to many of us as breathing. Yet all the while, a nagging feeling deep in our hearts and souls tells us something very wrong is happening.[2]

The relationship dynamics are somewhat different when our difficult person is not our adult child, but there is nonetheless a similarity in many interpersonal relationships when it comes to unclear and unhealthy boundaries. Ask yourself two questions as you begin to identify the core challenges in your relationships with difficult people. At the end of chapter 1, I asked you to have a notebook handy. Write down the answers to these questions:

1. Have I enabled their repeated inappropriate behavior? How so?
2. Am I helping them to avoid the consequences they need to experience?

Low Self-Esteem

"People with low self-esteem have their major difficulties in relationships with others. They don't properly value themselves. Therefore, they look for external things or people to give them value. They then become enslaved to the way others perceive them," said Bernis Riley.

This is because they're unable to establish healthy boundaries with people. Low self-esteem opens the door to a variety of irrational thoughts, emotions, and actions that lead people to lose themselves in relationships with others. In turn, this absorption of self into others leads to a loss of personal internal control. People with low self-esteem have weakened internal controls and become dependent on strong external controls. They become controlled by the way others think about them, feel about them, and act toward them. People with low self-esteem depend on others' approval and recognition and are therefore fearful of rejection and conflict. It has been estimated in the self-esteem literature that more than 90 percent of us are suffering from low self-esteem to some degree.

A FEW CHARACTERISTICS OF LOW SELF-ESTEEM

- irrational responses, ruled by negative thoughts and feelings
- perfectionism, fear of failure and of making mistakes
- suspicion and defensiveness

- jealousy and envy, feeling unlovable and unworthy
- fear of abandonment and of being hurt
- fear of change
- self-deprecation, shame, and a tendency to blame and criticize
- dependencies, codependency, addictions, eating disorders, and other disorders
- excessive worry, fear, and anxiety
- lack of confidence
- lack of purpose in life, no direction, confusion
- people pleasing and looking for constant approval

Codependency

Codependency is a learned behavior that can be passed down from one generation to another. It's an emotional and behavioral condition that affects an individual's ability to have a healthy, mutually satisfying relationship. It's also known as *relationship addiction* because people with codependency often form or maintain relationships that are one-sided, emotionally destructive, and sometimes abusive. The disorder was first identified as the result of years of studying interpersonal relationships in families of alcoholics. Codependent behavior is learned by watching and imitating other family members who display this type of behavior.

Codependents have low self-esteem and look for anything outside of themselves to make them feel better. They find it hard to be themselves. Some try to feel better through alcohol, drugs, or nicotine and become addicted. Others may develop compulsive behaviors, such as workaholism, gambling, or indiscriminate sexual activity.

These people have good intentions. They try to take care of people who are experiencing difficulty, but the caregiving becomes compulsive and defeating. Codependents often take on a martyr's role and become benefactors to individuals in need. A wife may cover for her alcoholic husband, a mother may make excuses for a truant child, or a father may pull some strings to keep his child from suffering the consequences of delinquent behavior.

The problem is that these repeated rescue attempts allow needy individuals to continue on their destructive course and to become even more dependent on the unhealthy caretaking of the benefactor. As this reliance increases, codependents develop a sense of reward and satisfaction from being needed. When the caretaking becomes compulsive, codependents feel helpless in the relationship, as if they have no choice, but they are unable to break away from the unhealthy cycle of behavior. Codependents view themselves as victims and are attracted to that same weakness in their love and friendship relationships. One respondent to my questionnaire wrote this:

> As a recovering codependent who struggles with setting boundaries, I would like to give a word of encouragement to others. We all know that we can only change ourselves and that we cannot change others. As you begin to set healthy boundaries, your difficult people will resist you every step of the way. It will definitely change your relationships, and not always for the better. Your difficult people probably will not embrace the changes you are making. But it will be worth it. In time, when they are forced to accept the new you, they may respect you for it or they may not. Whatever the outcome, you will be a healthier you. You may not gain approval from them, but you will from the One whose approval really matters.

A Few Characteristics of Codependent People

- an exaggerated sense of responsibility for the actions of others
- a tendency to confuse love and pity, and a tendency to "love" people they can pity and rescue
- a tendency to do more than their share, all of the time
- a tendency to become hurt when people don't recognize their efforts

- an unhealthy dependence on relationships, a willingness to do anything to hold on to a relationship and avoid the feeling of abandonment
- an extreme need for approval and recognition
- a sense of guilt when asserting themselves
- a compelling need to control others
- difficulty identifying feelings
- rigidity and difficulty adjusting to change
- problems with intimacy and boundaries

THE DIFFERENCE BETWEEN CODEPENDENCY AND ENABLING

It's sometimes difficult to understand the difference between these words. Codependency is a psychological condition in which a person is controlled or manipulated by another who is affected with a pathological condition (such as an addiction to alcohol or heroin).

Enabling is providing the means or opportunity to make something possible or easy, or to give legal power, capacity, or sanction to something or someone. These traits can exist separately or in tandem. Bernis gives us more of an understanding of the difference.

> Codependency is the underlying condition, the state of being, the motivation that drives the enabling behavior; enabling is the actual behavior of "helping" the offender. For instance, a woman who enables her alcoholic husband may make excuses to the husband's boss for missed work. This behavior is driven by a codependent mind-set that says her husband needs her to help him out of this predicament, and if she doesn't, she will be the one to suffer even greater consequences.

The Need to Please

Bernis says this about the need to please.

> This is often referred to as *subjugation*, which is another way of saying that someone is excessively compliant. Because they

need to please others in order to feel good about themselves, people who rely on subjugation as a style of relating surrender control to others. They often fear punishment or abandonment. Through life experiences they have come to think that their needs and feelings are not valid or important to others.

TRAITS ASSOCIATED WITH SUBJUGATION

- passive-aggressive behaviors, such as agreeing to do something but not following through
- uncontrolled outbursts of anger
- a feeling of being bullied
- feeling powerless
- having no control or say
- not feeling allowed to have an opinion
- suppressing of thoughts, opinions, or feelings to avoid punishment
- feeling ashamed or guilty for speaking up

The Need for Approval

Bernis explains this need.

> The need for approval is a God-given need. We look for approval in our relationships with significant others, especially our parents. Parents who are disapproving or critical and judgmental give children a sense of never being good enough, so these children grow up with the idea that approval for who they are depends on how well they achieve or succeed. Parents who give approval for things that are not true measures of achievement give their children a false sense of what is necessary for success.

> These children often grow up with a sense of entitlement and an inflated estimation of their abilities. Romans 12:3 says that we are to not think more highly of ourselves than we ought to

think, but we are to think about ourselves accurately. People who need to please and people who need approval focus on getting approval to feel good about themselves, and their sense of approval depends on the reactions of other people rather than on the truth about their worth and value. Their sense of worth and value is based on the opinion of others rather than on who they truly are.

People who have this need will work hard at being good—at their job, in their home life, with their spouse, as parents, and as adult children with their own parents. They are people pleasers, doing, acting, and being for others what they think the others want. They will do anything to avoid hurting the feelings of others, even if it means swallowing their own feelings or denying the reality of things. These people fear rejection, neglect, abandonment, and disapproval so much that they give up their own wants, needs, and rights, subjecting themselves to the wants, needs, and whims of others.

Traits Associated with the Need for Approval

- waiting for others' permission to give themselves recognition for what they do
- depending on others to give them a sense of self-worth
- poor ability to solve problems
- avoidance of conflict for fear that others will not approve of their point of view
- working hard to keep peace at any price
- difficulty letting others know how they think or feel about things
- a tendency to be overly responsible, taking on the responsibility of others to get things done
- a lack of self-confidence in their skills, abilities, and knowledge; a tendency to see themselves as incompetent

A History of Abuse

Bernis addresses this issue often in her private practice. Here's what she has to say.

> Abuse is a blatant violation of boundaries. It crosses all physical, mental, emotional, and psychological boundaries. Abuse not only violates another person's boundaries but also causes a deep wounding of the soul. If left untreated, this wound becomes infected with anger, bitterness, resentment, fear, disappointment, and self-loathing. If you are a survivor of abuse, whether as a child or as an adult, counseling is recommended to help you find healing for your wounds of abuse.

As someone who has personally experienced extreme physical violence, I know the damage this violation of boundaries can do to virtually every area of our lives. My relationship with the Lord has brought healing and hope to my life, and it's been decades since I've experienced domestic abuse, but the effects left lasting impressions.

Characteristics of Victims of Abuse

- easily angered, agitated, or upset
- extreme anxiety or panic without warning
- negative or pessimistic outlook on life
- a sense of impending doom
- problems identifying feelings
- inability or fear of expressing intimacy
- difficulty expressing needs or wants
- feeling worthless

Assess the Danger

Before we go any further, if someone has violated a physical boundary and you fear for your safety or the safety of someone you are responsible for (such as a child or an aging parent), remove yourself and your loved ones from the situation *immediately* and seek the help of legal authorities. There is no excuse for physical violence, and you alone must set the boundary for zero tolerance of physical abuse.

Identify the Problems

Any relationship involves certain mutual needs, requirements, and expectations. Things like love, respect, and responsibility should be happening in a good, meaningful flow between two people for the relationship to be functioning. What are the specific things that are interrupting that flow? Make a list of the specific challenges you are experiencing with the difficult person in your life. It's important to clearly state the specific issues; otherwise, the situation can become so broad and general that nothing effective can ever be done. To say "He's an idiot" or "She's crazy" may help you blow off steam, but it won't help you focus on what's really going on, and more importantly, it won't help you set a healthy boundary. Write the issues down in your notebook. Here are some examples.

- My best friend at church gossips about everyone.
- I can't depend on my ex-husband to be reliable and responsible.
- My coworker steals office supplies.
- My husband hits me.
- My sister is a chronic enabler and interferes in my life.
- My boyfriend is jealous of every friend I have.
- A neighbor has a dog that barks almost 24/7.
- My ex-wife makes custody issues a nightmare.
- My roommate leaves the doors unlocked and windows open when he leaves the house.
- My father-in-law swears profusely around my young children.

- My husband watches Internet pornography every day.
- My adult child is addicted to drugs, and his lifestyle causes drama, chaos, and crisis.

As I've said, that last example speaks to my life. By the time I hit my midthirties, my adult son was the primary difficult person in my life, and I related to him and his choices in some pretty unhealthy ways. I loved my son and desired to help him, yet I was motivated a great deal of the time by fear and guilt—fear of what would happen to him if I didn't come to his rescue, and guilt that I had been a poor parent and role model when he was a child.

Other motivating factors in my life had nothing to do with my son but were rooted in emotions and pain from my past—things I had never quite come to terms with. In many ways, my thinking was more than a bit off, especially concerning boundaries and balance. Dr. Laura addresses this kind of thing in her book *Bad Childhood, Good Life.*

> Early coping and defensive strategies often become habits, and habits are behaviors that are reflexive, repetitive, and without much conscious thought. People generally do not recognize that their current behaviors were perhaps suited to their childhood circumstances, but not their immediate situations or relationships. That's why these behaviors and ways of thinking and interpreting events and others' intentions are unusually "off," not constructive, and annoying to others.[3]

John Townsend offers this encouragement: "Stay with the main, big-picture actions and attitudes that put you in jeopardy, are ruining the relationship, keep you up at night, and generally permeate your life in a negative way. This is a war, though hopefully it is a war of love. So pick the battles that matter most."[4]

Name the Difficult People

Right relationships can fill our lives with joy, comfort, and satisfaction. Conversely, wrong relationships can burden our hearts with sadness, pain, and confusion. Quite often, one relationship triggers both kinds of feelings. Such can be the nature of relationships, particularly when we have not established or communicated our need for healthy boundaries.

Some relationships are more complex than others, especially those closest to our core. (We'll talk about our concentric circles of concern in part 3.)

If difficult people are causing serious problems, they most likely hold positions of value or influence in your life, making the situations all the more serious, all the more painful.

Rate the Level of Severity

You've recognized your contribution, addressed your personal issues, identified the problems, and named the difficult people in your life. Now, using John Townsend's four criteria mentioned earlier, let's identify how serious your issues are. Write the corresponding number next to the problems you have listed.

1. mildly irritating
2. causing disruptions in intimacy and love
3. creating family chaos
4. causing damage or danger

Boundaries play a significant role in everyone's daily life, and yet the subject of how and when to set healthy ones often remains confusing, particularly when a relationship has taken a turn for the worse. Perhaps that is where you're at today. Perhaps you're dealing with a difficult situation or circumstance but not necessarily a difficult person.

Get your notebook and review the names you've already written down. Then ask yourself, "Are these truly difficult people, or is it the situation that has become difficult?"

SANITY Support

1. Did you identify with any of the personal issues covered in this chapter? If so, which ones?

2. Is there a personal issue not mentioned in the chapter that you struggle with and that interferes with setting healthy boundaries?

3. Fear will interfere with your ability to set healthy boundaries. What specifically are you afraid will happen if you set boundaries with your difficult person?

4. What does Proverbs 4:23 mean to you?

5

Addressing Emotions

A man on his Harley was riding along a California beach when suddenly the sky clouded above his head and in a booming voice God said, "Because you have tried to be faithful to Me in all ways, I will grant you one wish." The biker pulled over and responded, "Build a bridge to Hawaii so I can ride over anytime I want."

God replied, "Your request is so materialistic! Think of the enormous challenges for that kind of undertaking, think of the steel it would take. I can do this, but it is hard for Me to justify your desire for worldly things. Take a minute and think of something that could possibly help mankind."

The biker thought for a moment, and finally he said, "Okay, I wish all men could understand women and their emotions, how they feel, what they are thinking, why they cry, what they mean when they say something is wrong, why they snap, and how to make them truly happy."

God replied, "You want two lanes or four on that bridge?"

Emotional Triggers

Emotions have perplexed men and women since the beginning of time. When it comes to dealing with difficult people, emotions play a critical role.

If you have a brother or sister who is driving you to drink, a coworker who has you considering quitting rather than dealing with her another day, an ex-spouse making child visitation a nightmare, or a friend from church whose habit of gossiping is actually keeping you from attending Sunday service, it's not going to be enough to simply construct a new personal boundary to protect yourself. Yes, that's a critical start, but you also need to gain a better understanding of your emotions—what you are thinking and feeling in your challenging relationship with this difficult person.

What emotional trigger is this difficult person pulling in the first place?

Why do some people simply rub us the wrong way? Is it because of a defect in our own character? Could our own filter need fixing? And what if we really do have a legitimate gripe? If the difficult people in our lives really are in the wrong, if they're the ones who need to change, what then?

Although it may appear that I'm beating a dead horse every time I repeat this sentiment, for many it bears repeating. It's not up to us to change or fix the difficult people in our lives; we need to shine light on our own stuff and get our own houses in order. We've got to reprogram our minds to understand that we are responsible only for our own choices, responses, and reactions, not theirs.

"But Allison, this person really is an imbecile. She drives everybody crazy—I'm not the only one who says so."

That may be so. Some difficult people are simply toxic, and the only way you can survive is to live without them in your life. But for the most part—and hear me please when I say this—difficult people are only going to cause us as much difficulty as we allow them to. We have far more control over our situations, circumstances, and emotions than we think. If we can understand why our bosses make the hair on our neck stand up every time they correct our performance, that increase in our self-awareness can go a long way to assist us in establishing healthy boundaries with them. The toxic boss doesn't go away, but when our toxic responses do, things change.

Our reactions say more about our own style of relating to others than about the other people. We need to develop an approach to troubling relationships that empowers the difficult people to change in positive ways and helps us change and grow also.

Let me clarify this. Our goal is not to change or fix someone else, but if something we say or do influences them to make a change, wouldn't that be a wonderful by-product? Isn't that the point of loving your neighbor?

Remember our higher calling—to love God and use that love to serve Him and others. We are called to be His witnesses. Unfortunately, many of us have neglected to focus on this truth, and our painful emotions have prompted us to make some misguided choices. We've developed unhealthy habits, allowing our emotions to be controlled by other people's attitudes and actions.

A habit is a pattern of behavior acquired by frequent repetition that reflects the prevailing character of a person. As Christians, our character should reflect the character of Christ.

We are not born with habits—we develop them. Perhaps it's time to learn more about the part our emotions play in our relationships with difficult people and then to develop new habits of emotional self-control.

Understanding Emotions

What are emotions for anyway? What do they do for us? They certainly have a significant effect on us, but what is it all for?

Emotions motivate us. Motivations are felt in the body. Our muscles tense or relax. Our blood vessels dilate or contract. When we feel something emotionally, we also have physical feelings. Our emotions can make us feel uncomfortable or comfortable, sending us signals to do something urgently or to stay in our comfortable state.

Motivations

I asked Bernis Riley to clarify this for us.

> Motivations are our goals, drives, desires, and needs. They often lie outside our conscious awareness. For that reason, they

are difficult to identify and even more difficult to manage and target for change. Psychological theories abound about what motivates people, and to date, all we can really say with certainty regarding motivation is that people are purposeful. Now, what they are purposeful about is difficult to determine.

Signals

When we're trying to understand something or make a decision, our emotions help us determine whether what we've concluded is a good idea. When we think about something that contradicts our values, our emotions will warn us of the conflict. When we think about something that could hurt us, our emotions will tell us this is not a good idea. Just imagining what might happen triggers our emotions, and that helps us make better decisions.

When emotions are used as social signals, they help others decide how to behave toward us and vice versa. This is generally very useful. If someone is looking angry, approaching him for a favor might not be a good idea. If someone is looking afraid, perhaps she needs help. We generally wear our hearts on our sleeves—our inner emotions are often displayed on our outer bodies. Our faces have about 90 muscles, 30 of which have the sole purpose of signaling emotions to other people, such as anger, sadness, fear, and joy.

There are more negative emotions than positive emotions. We can feel fear, anger, shame, hate, and many other unpleasant feelings, yet beyond a basic happiness and joy, there are few other positive feelings. One reason for this is that most emotions are designed to keep us alive. They signal warnings and prompt us to act—to run away from danger or to fight back. Without emotions we would not survive.

Emotions are signals that tell us something about what is happening in our inner person. This can be very useful because we don't realize what's going on in our subconscious. Becoming more aware of our own emotions and emotional triggers can go a long way in helping us better understand what makes us tick.

For example, Margaret had a new boss who managed to grate on her last nerve whenever he spoke and especially when he corrected her work—which was often. He was the difficult person who made her life miserable. Apparently she couldn't do anything right for him. She had begun to practice role-playing a conversation in which she set a boundary—she was going to quit. But before she could get the words out, he beat her to the punch and set a boundary with her first. This prompted a Spirit-filled epiphany.

> As crazy as it sounds, I never made the connection that my new boss reminded me of my father, a man who was never pleased with anything I did and who died a bitter, lonely old man. Not that my boss looks anything like him, he doesn't. In fact, he's a young, educated guy with a lot of people skills—nothing at all like my dad. Initially, I was taken aback when he called me into his office to tell me that my defensive responses to his requests were becoming increasingly problematic for him and our team and that I risked losing my job if things continued as they were.
>
> So I stepped back to look at the big picture, and it made sense. It was the act of being corrected that set me off. But the fact is, my boss wouldn't have needed to correct me as often if I had listened to his instructions in the first place. I began to realize that I was making his job harder simply because the emotions that bubbled up when he corrected me took me to a place that made me defensive, irrational, and confrontational. The bottom line was that he was right. I wasn't following his directions, and *I* was the one who needed to change, not him. I didn't need to quit my job; I needed to quit my own destructive patterns of responding to him. It was like night and day when I made the choice to actually listen to his instructions and follow them. Today, we're a great team, and it's because I managed to rein in my emotions and not let them control me.

The Emotions That Drive Us

Drs. Cloud and Townsend believe we often fail to set boundaries because we have false motives for doing what we do in the first place.

We often give (or "help") for all the wrong reasons, and after closer scrutiny, we will often find that our motive for giving was not love, but the fear of losing love.

For example, we might say, "I'm helping my daughter with (fill in the blank) because I love her." But if we listened to our emotions, we might more accurately say, "I'm helping my daughter (fill in the blank) because if I don't, she won't love me and will probably move out of the house, and I'm afraid to be alone." Or we might say, "I'm going to bail my brother out of jail again because I love him." But our emotions might lead us to the truth: "I'm going to bail my brother out of jail again because if I don't, my mom and dad will never forgive me."

Many parents are discovering that the reasons they have enabled their adult children for so long are not based on loving or helping. In fact, the reasons rooted deep within those parents often have almost nothing whatsoever to do with their adult children. Instead, they are related to the parents' own emotional triggers.

The same can be true for those of us dealing with difficult people. Because of our emotional triggers, our motives for not setting healthy boundaries in the first place are often based on our own emotions:

- fear of abandonment or loss of love
- fear of others' anger
- fear of loneliness
- fear of losing the good me inside
- fear of consequences
- guilt
- revenge and the desire for payback
- longing for approval
- inappropriate identification with others' loss

We do many of the things we do because we feel guilty, need approval, or want revenge. We do these things because "it's what they deserve" or because we're afraid they'll get mad if we don't. We do things because we don't want someone we love to experience pain or loss. It's impossible to list every false motive, but they are all distortions of our God-given need to love and be loved.

Difficult People Have Emotions Too

In order to obey God's commandment to love our neighbors, we need to consider the perspective of the difficult people in our lives. Having empathy includes understanding that these people have feelings and emotions of their own. Unless we've walked in their shoes, we have no idea where they are coming from or what's weighing on their hearts. In such cases, we need empathy for the other person.

Empathy is different from sympathy. Being sympathetic means having pity and feeling sorry for other people. But when we have empathy, we can truly understand (or at least imagine) the depth of people's feelings. We feel *with* people rather than feel sorry *for* people.

Feeling true empathy can be more than a little challenging when someone is causing us pain and stress. Challenging, yes, but with God's help, not impossible.

If we have trouble setting boundaries, chances are we have our own issues to deal with, and it's important that we deal with them. Remember God's plan in Proverbs 4:23: "Above all else, guard your heart, for everything you do flows from it." Protecting yourself and not becoming entangled in the emotional state of the difficult person in your life can become tricky. Sometimes you need to maintain distance even when practicing empathy. Having empathy does not mean allowing people to mistreat us.

Author John Townsend writes about a woman he knows:

> I have a friend who has severe problems that sometimes affect her friends and family in negative ways. She suffers from a very long background of severe trauma, abuse, and neglect that most of us can't imagine. She has had financial, emotional, relational, and medical problems that have been profound, some of them related to her background, and some not. She has worked hard on this most of her life, diligently growing

and changing. She has made major changes. But still her condition has been very troubling.

Thus, what she deals with at times affects those around her. Sometimes she will withdraw from life, and her support group will call her or visit her to keep her connected. Sometimes she has intense emotional outbursts, and those in her life must deal with them. Sometimes she has crisis, and people who love her stay with her until it is resolved.

But she really isn't a button-pusher. She has worked harder in her personal growth than most people I know. She has given up more than most of us know. She loves God in a very deep and personal way. She cares about her friends and hates it when she is a burden to them. She tries to help others with what resources she has.

I know one thing: her friends never resent her. They may feel drained by the demand that her problems bring to them, but they don't blame her. They never feel that she is taking advantage of their kindness, or that she isn't doing her part. In fact, sometimes they have to tell her, "Look, call us when you're in trouble. We don't like it when you shut us out."

And I know another thing: her struggles, by nature, are very, very different from her former ones. There are some people whose progress you cannot evaluate until you look at where they've come from. When you see where she has been, you marvel at the change.[1]

Although I've been blessed to meet Dr. Townsend numerous times and to learn from him in several small group seminars, I'm relatively certain I'm not the friend he describes. Yet I wept as I read his words. In many ways, I felt I could be that woman.

Everyone has a past. Some more colorful than others, ranging from pitiful to privileged, from tremendous to tragic. Because of the emotional baggage we carry, some of us get temporarily stuck when we're confronted with challenging relationships. We react negatively and perpetuate the dysfunctional cycle. Take heed—the individual you think is a difficult person may be thinking the same about you. Many of us who have difficult people in our lives can in fact be difficult people in our own right.

The New Testament book of Ephesians includes this powerful Scripture passage to cling to:

> So Christ himself gave the apostles, the prophets, the evangelists, the pastors and teachers, to equip his people for works of service, so that the body of Christ may be built up until we all reach unity in the faith and in the knowledge of the Son of God and become mature, attaining to the whole measure of the fullness of Christ.
>
> Then we will no longer be infants, tossed back and forth by the waves, and blown here and there by every wind of teaching and by the cunning and craftiness of people in their deceitful scheming. Instead, speaking the truth in love, we will grow to become in every respect the mature body of him who is the head, that is, Christ. From him the whole body, joined and held together by every supporting ligament, grows and builds itself up in love, as each part does its work (Ephesians 4:11-16).

An Emotional Checkup

As you continue to do the work needed to mature, stop for a moment and ask yourself, "How well have I established and maintained my emotional boundaries in my relationships?"

Learning to set healthy boundaries can feel uncomfortable and even scary because it may go against the grain of the survival skills we learned in childhood—particularly if our caregivers were physically, sexually, or emotionally abusive. For example, we may have learned to repress our anger or other painful emotions because we would have been attacked and blamed for expressing the very pain the abuse had caused. Thus, attempting to set healthy boundaries as adults may initially be accompanied by anxiety, but we must learn to work through these conditioned fears, or we will never have healthy relationships.

We must ask God to help us address our own emotions and

motivations and to open our hearts to feel empathy for the difficult people in our lives.

At first, the choice to make deliberate and rational responses when someone trips an emotional trigger will seem awkward. In time that feeling will change. If God is our plumb line; eventually, the pendulum will come back to rest at the center.

Once again, you can feel empathy for someone while still setting a boundary.

If you need to strengthen your boundaries with the difficult people in your life to enrich or regain the health of your relationships, thoughtfully consider the questions below. Take your time—this exercise can be more helpful than you might think. I encourage you to write your answers in your notebook. Many of us have never taken the time to conduct an emotional self-assessment. We're often too busy being emotional!

SANITY Support

1. What basic emotion motivates you to respond the way you do to the difficult person in your life? What do you gain and what do you lose by using this emotional response?

2. How successfully do you protect and maintain your boundaries when difficult people are highly intrusive and persistent?

3. Do you use unhealthy, compulsive, or addictive behaviors as barriers or unhealthy boundaries to protect yourself from intimacy with your difficult person?

4. How well do you stay unhooked and detached when your difficult person is testing your boundaries in the relationship?

5. Does your inability to maintain healthy intellectual,

emotional, physical, and spiritual boundaries within any relationship frighten you?

6. When you consider trying to maintain healthy boundaries in your relationships without the use of body weight, food, or some other compulsive behaviors to protect and medicate yourself, are you scared?

7. Would you prefer to continue using your unhealthy distancing techniques or to learn how to establish healthy boundaries with your difficult person?

6

Tracking the Temperaments

Why do different people cope with similar life experiences in different ways? For example, two children with the same abusive parents may respond very differently. One becomes a passive, frightened victim and remains that way throughout life. The other child becomes openly rebellious and defiant and may even leave home early to survive as a teenager on the streets.

This is partly because we have different temperaments at birth. Temperamentally, we may tend to be more frightened or aggressive, outgoing or shy. Our natural temperaments push us in certain directions.

Another reason may be that we unconsciously choose different parents to copy or model ourselves after. For example, because an abuser often marries a victim, a child in this family could model the abusive parent or the victimized parent or some characteristics of both.

One thing is for sure: By the time we reach adulthood, we have become conglomerations of elements. Our personalities have been molded by circumstances, the environment, coping styles, emotions, motivations, experiences, influences, and yes, our choices. However, whatever the years may bring, our natural temperaments remain.

Four Personality Types

The Greek physician Hippocrates described four basic temperaments

400 years before Christ was born. Florence Littauer, the founder of Christian Leaders, Authors, and Speakers Seminars (CLASS) and the author of the bestselling book *Personality Plus*, puts her own imprint on the four original temperaments.

> We were all born with our own temperament traits, our raw material, our own kind of rock. Some of us are granite, some marble, some alabaster, some sandstone. Our type of rock doesn't change, but our shapes can be altered. So it is with our personalities. We start with our own set of inborn traits. Some of our qualities are beautiful with strains of gold. Some are blemished with fault lines of gray. Our circumstances, IQ, nationality, economics, environment, and parental influences can mold our personalities, but the rock underneath remains the same.[1]

Florence explains that understanding the differences in our basic temperaments takes the pressure off our human relationships. She says life will change when we can look at each other's differences in a positive way and not try to make everyone be like us. She identifies two critical things about the temperaments that can change our lives.

1. We must examine our own strengths and weaknesses and learn how to accentuate our positives and eliminate our negatives.

2. We must understand other people and realize that just because others are different does not make them wrong.

How liberating! Just think, all those things difficult people do to send us over the edge (and vice versa) may simply be expressions of their "raw material," and once we understand them better (that is, we empathize with them), we'll be able to communicate our boundaries more effectively.

There are four temperaments:

As per Hippocrates	As per Florence Littauer
sanguine	popular sanguine
choleric	powerful choleric
phlegmatic	peaceful phlegmatic
melancholic	perfect melancholy

If you know anything about the four temperaments, you don't need to be around me long to see I'm a "powerful choleric"—a dominant personality. We're known to be leaders, organizers, and communicators—goal-oriented but not necessarily relationship-oriented. This doesn't mean I don't need (or want) relationships. It just means that the way I perceive and develop them is different from the way other personality types do. Remember, every temperament has both strengths and weaknesses.

This is important self-knowledge to possess, especially when we're looking at what motivates us to do the things we do. What makes us have boundary-related problems in the first place? Could some of the aspects of our inborn temperament predispose us to respond to others in a certain way? If so, what can we do to accentuate the positive and tone down the negative?

Unfortunately, learning about the personality temperaments was about as important as learning "Boundary Setting 101" when most of us were growing up. These were not things we were taught.

Do you know your personality type? Your strengths and weaknesses? If not, I encourage you to do some reading on this topic. You don't need to become a specialist about this, but insights into the strengths and weaknesses of your personality can be valuable knowledge to possess.

I'm aware that as a result of my powerful personality type, life experiences, and influences, I can often appear overly forceful, especially to people with more subdued personality traits. Additionally, because of the abuse I've experienced in my past, I can sometimes get defensive, sidetracked, and even confused in my relationships. It takes me more time than some to figure out the obvious. I pray often for God not only to soften my sharp edges but also to give me wisdom and discernment concerning my friendships.

I have a friend who is very much like me. Her energy bounces off the walls like fireflies caught in a jar. I've heard some people say, "I can't imagine working with someone like her," but I personally find her wonderfully energizing to be around—we get so much accomplished! Do we often butt heads? Yes. But our relationship has helped me to be not only a better friend but also a better person.

Building strong relationships isn't a passive exercise. It doesn't automatically happen because you want it to. It takes involvement, commitment, willingness to be vulnerable, and a keen understanding that whatever situation we find ourselves in today is not a surprise to God. He has a plan for every relationship that He orchestrates. Even our difficult ones.

This could be the single most vital teaching we need to wrap our brains around—that God indeed has a plan.

A Different Perspective

It's important to remember that the way some people may feel about you and your communication style (or personality temperament) might be the polar opposite of what someone else may feel, and that doesn't necessarily mean you are wrong.

For example, one of my dearest friends recently told me one of the things she admires and respects the most about me is that I speak up when something is bothering me.

"I always know where I stand with you," she said, "I can trust that about you, and I like that kind of dependability in our friendship. I admire you for who you are."

This was encouraging because a few days earlier I overheard a woman I barely knew say quite the opposite about me. Perhaps I reminded this woman of someone or something that flipped an emotional trigger that had very little to do with me personally, or maybe our inherent personality types were quite the opposite.

That didn't stop me from wanting to defend myself. But the truth is, we cannot be everything to everybody. We need to own who we are, whose we are, and where we come from. As we embrace the most important relationship in life and grow in God's grace, we must pray that God will help mold and shape us into the people He wants us to be.

Let's pray for wisdom and discernment to approach the subject of emotions and temperament in a way that honors God, protects our hearts, and allows us to love our neighbors. Let's pray that our earthly relationships will become healthier, more loving, and less difficult.

"Blessed are the peacemakers, for they will be called children of God" (Matthew 5:9).

SANITY Support

1. Think about the difficult relationships you have. Write out how your personality or temperament differs from those in your difficult relationships.

2. Though we might say that it is okay for everyone to be unique, to be different, the reality is that our differences are often at the root of our relational difficulties. What differences create difficulty with these people in your life?

3. If we are going to get along with others, we must accept that we all have our own unique perspective on the events of our lives. Can you think of a time when not accepting this reality has kept you from being at peace with someone who did not agree with your perspective? Write out what you would say or do differently if you could go back and relive that interaction.

7

Confronting Anger

In response to my questionnaire, A.M. from Ohio talked candidly about how she typically responds to people who have overstepped her boundaries.

> If someone criticizes me, my first reaction is to lash out. I know it's wrong and regret it the second it happens. I cringe to hear the words coming out of my mouth. Yet still, I lash out more often than not. I am surrounded by others who don't care about anyone but themselves. They do the least amount of work to get by and then whine about how they can't afford this or that. Yet when I see them at the grocery store, they have beer and cigarettes in their cart. This drives my own anger through the roof, and though I try to tell myself that I can only control me, some days I want to get in their faces and scream, "Give up the booze and cigarettes and maybe you'll be able to buy fruit!"
>
> Of course, this would probably get me punched at the least, shot at the most. I find that anger seems to be playing tug-of-war with selfishness in people more and more with every generation. Very few of us think of others first.

It is not a sin to be angry. Anger is a God-given emotion. But we sometimes express our anger in sinful ways. The apostle Paul warns us about this: "'In your anger do not sin.' Do not let the sun go down while you are still angry, and do not give the devil a foothold" (Ephesians 4:26-27).

Anger is a signal that something is wrong. When we feel that our rights have been violated, we often respond with anger. Instead of verbally communicating our needs and establishing healthy boundaries so that whatever has occurred does not occur again, we often lash out, as A.M. testifies.

Anger can also be a protective wall that keeps people away. In her book *The Dance of Anger: A Woman's Guide to Changing the Patterns of Intimate Relationships,* author Harriet Lerner writes about two styles of managing anger that appear to be as different as night and day. Yet upon closer inspection, they both protect others, blur our clarity of self, and ensure that change does not occur. Both styles have boundary issues at their core.

In essence, the "good girl" style is when our primary energy is directed toward...preserving harmony at all costs, and not rocking any boats. Anger of any kind is repressed. In other words, good girls keep as quiet as possible, setting and enforcing as few boundaries as possible. However, the more "nice" we are, the more we accumulate a storehouse of unconscious anger and rage, and while the real issues go unaddressed, we may become less and less of an expert about our own thoughts, feelings and wants. We don't want to be called selfish, egocentric, rebellious, unfeminine, neurotic, or controlling, so instead we feel hurt, guilty and often depressed.

Conversely, the "bad girl" style is when we know we are angry and do speak up, a behavior that brings a host of often unfair definitions.

> Obviously, it requires courage to know when we are angry and to let others hear about it. The problem occurs when we are stuck in a pattern of ineffective fighting, complaining, and blaming that only preserves the status quo. When this happens, we unwittingly protect others at our own expense. On the one hand, an angry woman is threatening. When we voice our anger ineffectively, however—without clarity, direction, and control—it may, in the end, be reassuring to others. We

allow ourselves to be written off and we provide others with an excuse not to take us seriously and hear what we are saying. Sometimes, the nature of our fighting or angry accusations may actually allow the other person to get off the hook.

Those of us who fight ineffectively are usually caught up in unsuccessful efforts to change a person who does not want to change. When our attempts to change the other person's beliefs, feelings, reactions, or behaviors do not work, we may then continue to do more of the same, reacting in predictable, patterned ways that only escalate the very problems we complain about. We may be so driven by emotionality that we do not reflect on our options for behaving differently or even believe that new options are possible. Thus, our fighting protects the old familiar patterns in our relationships as surely as does the silence of "nice ladies" [aka: the good girls].

[Despite their radically different appearance,] after all is said and done—or *not* said and done—the outcome is the same; we are left feeling helpless and powerless. We do not feel in control of the quality and direction of our lives. Our sense of dignity and self-esteem suffers because we have not effectively clarified and addressed the real issues at hand. And nothing changes.[1]

Remember, being in control of the quality of your life is not the same as being controlling. And the good-girl or bad-girl differentiations can translate to men as well. We all know at least one good guy who doesn't want to speak up or a bad guy who seems to be the loud-mouthed bully. Is it possible that unhealthy boundaries—either too rigid or too loose—could be core motivators in both instances?

I admit that I often fall into the bad-girl category. My head understands the need to speak up and establish clear and healthy boundaries in a loving manner, but my emotions frequently get caught up in the mix. Unfortunately, in some instances I'm painfully aware of what Harriet Lerner means when she says we can "get stuck in a pattern of ineffective fighting, complaining, and blaming that only preserves the status quo."

There are difficult people in my life who make me angry—but I am never more angry at them than I am with myself for getting angry in the first place. I should know better. Why do I lapse into old habits that I know are unhealthy? Why has it taken so many years to learn these life lessons?

Harriet Lerner wrote, "Sometimes staying stuck is what we need to do until the time comes when we are confident that it is safe to get unstuck."[2]

For many of us, just admitting we are angry will be enough to propel us to the next stage, where true healing can begin—where we begin to make deliberate choices to change our responses. June Hunt writes, "Unresolved anger is a bed of hidden coals burning deep wounds into your relationships with God and others. This powerful emotion robs your heart of peace and steals contentment from your spirit."[3]

Whether you are a nice girl (or guy) or a bad girl (or guy), if unresolved anger exists in your heart, it's time to release it now. Finding SANITY is possible only when we address our anger appropriately. In many cases, successfully dealing with anger will mean crossing the often painful road to forgiveness.

SANITY Support

1. Rate your current level of anger with your difficult person on a scale of 1 (still waters) to 10 (volcano erupting).

2. Imagine the difficult person responding negatively to you. Where would you rate your anger now using the scale from question 1? What issues did this person trigger in you?

3. Do you have the good girl (or guy) style of conveying anger or the bad girl (or guy) style of conveying anger? Who in your family of origin had this same style of anger?

Choosing to Change

There is no doubt whatsoever that we can sometimes initiate change. However, some things will change with or without our involvement or consent, such as the weather or the seasons.

Choice, on the other hand, requires a conscious decision—our active participation.

We always have a choice. Therefore, change and choice go hand in hand.

I have often had heated discussions about this topic with someone who is a caregiver for a disabled individual. In my opinion, she often enables this person to the extreme. This topic has surfaced often over the years as she counters back that she does not enable—she does what "she has to do" and has no choice. "It's my responsibility, my obligation," she insists. "I have no choice."

I argue that she does in fact have a choice. She chooses to feel obligated. That's her choice, but it *is* a choice.

Whether we are being responsible or irresponsible, loving or angry, caring or rude, we behave and respond to life's situations the way we do not because we are genetically programmed to do so, but because we *choose* to.

When Change Comes Down to Choice

Some people feel utterly powerless over their lives. This typically occurs when they feel they have no choice whatsoever in a matter, that things are happening to them over which they have no control.

The truth is, feeling powerless is in fact a choice. In reality, people choose to assume the role of one who has no choices—who is powerless.

If you're serious about putting an end to your ineffective and unhealthy responses to the difficult person in your life, it's fully within your power to make the choices that will change your life. You begin by asking God to help you do so. The more intimately we draw to the heart of God, the more clearly we know His will. Even though all choices may be permissible, some may not be the best.

We Have the Power and the Choice

We need to acknowledge that we're *not* in this present place of confusion and pain because of the difficult people in our lives. We're in this place because of the ways we have chosen to react and respond to them. Sometimes we made those choices unconsciously, passively accepting what may have *seemed* our only choice.

With an intellect and straightforward style I admire and respect, Dr. Laura Schlessinger has keen insight on this topic of choice. I think she is a brilliant communicator with an uncanny ability to quickly assess a situation and cut to the heart of an issue. She's not trying to win any popularity contests, and her advice is often raw, but it's seldom wrong.

Dr. Laura devotes many of her books and on-air radio time to people who make poor choices, people who are caught up in the bubble of insanity, repeating the same behavior and expecting different results. This is particularly true when people have experienced an early childhood trauma. She writes this in her book *Bad Childhood, Good Life: How to Blossom and Thrive in Spite of an Unhappy Childhood*:

> While there has been a whole cottage industry dedicated to those who believe and identify themselves as injured or handicapped by their childhoods—commonly known as *victim, survivor, adult child of,* or those with *low self-esteem,* or from a *dysfunctional family*—I believe that many people don't even realize that their childhood history *has* impacted their adult

thought and behavioral patterns in unproductive ways. They don't realize that some of their less pleasant or destructive adult emotional reactions are reflexive responses forged by their unfortunate childhood challenges. They don't realize that much of their adult life has been dedicated to repeating ugly childhood dynamics in an attempt to repair deep childhood hurts and longings. They're reduced to believing that neither they nor life matters much anyway, not understanding that they have the power and the choice to make a good life.[1]

Rational Choices Are Void of Excuses

A big issue we have regarding change and choice is our tendency to make excuses (to ourselves and others) for not changing. Excuses keep us in bondage, separated from any real resolution for the relationship problems we may be experiencing. Excuses may also keep the difficult people in our lives trapped in a place where they are not held responsible for their actions, a place where logical consequences are denied.

The excuses must end. We'll talk more about this in the *N* step in SANITY—nip excuses in the bud!

At this point, you may be thinking, "Allison, please don't make me feel even guiltier about my choices. I feel bad enough already."

I totally understand. However, if you really want to get your life back, things have to change. It's time to stop feeling guilty and start making positive changes. Take the spotlight off the situation and focus ownership of the issue squarely on your own shoulders.

Dr. Laura is a vocal advocate about making positive choices to regain the power in our lives that we have given away. We must make these positive choice regardless of what we may have experienced on the journey.

> While I suppose it is possible to sometimes make the case that a person was so traumatized and at such a vulnerable time in their lives that it became impossible for them to ever be happy or functional, I don't buy it. I do buy that it is a lot harder for some, due to their particular personality traits or magnitude of childhood problems, than others to take back

their opportunities and potential. While I was in private practice, I saw people I thought were so damaged that perhaps they could not possibly pull a positive life together. I would sit, week after week, in awe of their grit and spirit in making the better (always scary) choices to improve their lives. Then there were the others who seemed to have so much going for them, with minimal external restraints, who almost seemed determined to not progress past the first chapter of their lives.

The obvious question is, "What makes some people hold on to being a victim and others choose to improve their lives?" The answer is control. When you are a perpetual victim, the past is in control of your present. When you are a conqueror, the present is controlled by your choices, in spite of the pain and the pull of your past.[2]

Changing Our Choices

Some of us have been caught up in the dance of dysfunction for years. But it's never too late to change if we want to. It's our choice to become conquerors.

In his book *Dealing with the CrazyMakers in Your Life*, Dr. David Hawkins sums this up artfully.

> You and I must be able to make choices freely. Unfortunately, if you have been struggling with crazy-makers in your life, you may be addicted—in a loose sense of the word—to these people. You may be obsessively bound up in trying to change them instead of focusing your heart and soul on loving God, letting Him change you, and giving you wisdom for better ways of dealing with the situation.[3]

Why Change?

Many of us have known for quite some time that the insanity in which we are living is not right. We know the relationships we have with these difficult people are less than we hope for, and they increase the stress in our lives and in the lives of those we love. We've been in pain for quite a while. However, we have not considered the fact that our disobedience to God's plan may be a contributing factor.

As we take time to better understand the road we've been traveling, and to stop, step back, and reflect on God's Word and His priorities for our lives, it's a good time to begin identifying specific ways we can change—ways we can choose different paths that will bring hope, healing, and peace to our lives.

Pastor Ryan Northcutt says, "It's not about our power, but about God's power in us. It's not how strong we are to make changes or to conquer our troubles, it's about how much we depend on the Lord for the power to help us stay strong."

Many of us have been praying for wisdom to know how to handle the difficult people in our lives. However, "handling" them may not be the issue. Difficult people often seem to have the power to make us lose perspective. So the better prayer may be, "Lord, please give me wisdom to know why this difficult person is in my life and what You want me to learn from this relationship."

God designed us so that good relationships draw out and encourage the best in us—love, encouragement, grace, forgiveness, and more. If that isn't happening, something is wrong. Kody Wetzold, the youth pastor at Fellowship of the Parks in Texas, offered this exhortation:

> As Christ followers we are called to be different, returning hate with love, retaliation with forgiveness, and anger and frustration with kindness and understanding. Every day we choose whether to let our identities in Christ be that of merely talk, or to step up to the plate and allow Christ to live through our daily actions. Who we should be in Christ has absolutely nothing to do with our fears, struggles, or frustration with certain individuals. We are constantly being given a chance to show the world that we serve a God who offers so much more. It's time we show them exactly what that is.

Making the Choice to Forgive

Leaving a painful or difficult past to create a future of hope and healing will often require extreme acts of forgiveness.

In his book *Healing from Family Rifts: Ten Steps to Finding Peace*

After Being Cut Off from a Family Member, Mark Sichel addressed the importance of releasing toxic feelings that can weigh us down.

> Whether or not we forgive, we still need to take steps to clear out our minds of obsessive over-involvement with others' transgressions. Forgiveness has to do with the relationship between you and the person you may feel has hurt you: you may or may not be able to grant it, depending on the severity of that hurt. However, in either case, you can let go of resentments, whose only real function is to keep us in a state of poisonous, negative, angry, and rageful all-consuming thoughts about a past we cannot change.[4]

Our relational struggles with difficult people run the gamut from a misunderstanding with a coworker to the betrayal of a family member. Yet God did not say, "Love your neighbors only when they are lovable." His mercy and grace is extended to all of us equally and does not depend on the level of wrongdoing (sin).

Making the choice to change ourselves and be more Christlike, coupled with the choice to forgive, can help us become the people God has created us to be.

In his book *Handling Difficult People*, John Townsend once again has expert advice regarding change.

> Difficult people can and do change, in deep and long-lasting ways, all the time. God has been in the business of changing difficult people for eons. The apostle Paul, who wrote much of the New Testament, said that before God transformed him, he himself had been "the worst of sinners" (1 Timothy 1:16).
>
> There are no guarantees of change, as people always have freedom to choose poorly. But it is good to have the right and full perspective here: Your button-pusher can be outgunned. There is a lot you can do, and a lot that God can do through you: "I know that you can do all things; no plan of yours can be thwarted" (Job 42:2). We are talking about God Himself on your side![5]

About Freedom and Forgiveness

The difficult step to reconciliation with a difficult person who has hurt you may take time. Pray for the Holy Spirit to soften your heart so this step can one day take place—even if the offender has wronged you, and even if the step is never reciprocated.

In her book *Stormie*, Stormie Omartian recounts the way God helped her to forgive her mother under the most extreme situations. As I read this powerful memoir, I began to understand how God can work to restore, redeem, and renovate broken hearts and souls.

> The most important thing to remember when it comes to forgiving is that forgiveness doesn't make the other person right, it makes you free. The best way to turn anger, bitterness, hatred, and resentment for someone into love is to pray for that person. God softens your heart when you do and brings wholeness into your life.[6]

Scripture teaches us what it means to love.

> Love is patient, love is kind. It does not envy, it does not boast, it is not proud. It does not dishonor others, it is not self-seeking, it is not easily angered, it keeps no record of wrongs. Love does not delight in evil but rejoices with the truth. It always protects, always trusts, always hopes, always perseveres (1 Corinthians 13:4-7).

As we continue the journey to setting boundaries with difficult people, never underestimate the power of God to change our lives and the lives of those we love. Some of the most important decisions we can make are not only to change the way we respond to difficult people but also to be the agents of change that God will use to change the world.

In his transformational book *The Hole in Our Gospel*, author and president of World Vision Richard Stearns stirs our hearts with these words:

> So far I have spent twenty-two chapters arguing the case that there is a hole in our gospel and that, as a result, we have

embraced a view of our faith that is far too tame. We have, in fact, reduced the gospel to a mere transaction involving the right beliefs rather than seeing in it the power to change the world. I have painted a picture of a world aflame with violence, poverty, injustice, disease, corruption, and human suffering— a world in need of revolution. But I have also attempted to make clear from Scripture that the whole gospel—the very social revolution Jesus intended as His kingdom unfolded "in earth as it is in heaven"—has been entrusted to us, those who claim to follow Christ. Jesus seeks a new world order in which this whole gospel, hallmarked by compassion, justice, and proclamation of the good news, becomes a reality, first in our hearts and minds, and then in the wider world through our influence. This is not a far-off and distant kingdom to be experienced only in the afterlife. Christ's vision was of a redeemed world order populated by redeemed people—*now*. To accomplish this, we are to be salt and light in a dark and fallen world, the "yeast" that leavens the whole loaf of bread (the whole of society). We are the ones God has called to be His church. It's up to us. *We* are to be the change.

But a changed world requires *change agents*, and change agents are people who have first been changed themselves.[7]

Are you ready to make the choice to change?

SANITY Support

1. This chapter makes the point that we need to focus on changing ourselves rather than focusing on changing other people. Is this hard for you to accept? Why or why not?

2. If you choose to change, what exactly in your life needs to change?

3. Who has wounded your heart? Have you forgiven them for wounding your heart and damaging the relationship?

4. If you choose to respond differently to your difficult person, what do you suppose will happen? Play out the scenario in your mind and write out possible outcomes.

5. What would be different about your life if you genuinely forgave the difficult person in your life?

6. Sometimes we forgive merely so we don't have to live with negative feelings, such as bitterness, hate, anger, and the like. But God desires that we forgive in order to reconcile with our offenders. Do you forgive to avoid negative feelings or criticism? Or do you forgive in order to see the offender reconciled to God and to you?

9

Moving Forward with Purpose

In *Being Christian*, Steve Arterburn writes, "Better to be driving a bus than get hit by a bus." Whenever possible, it's good to be in the driver's seat, propelling our lives toward established goals. We do not want to have someone else control what happens to us. This can be especially true when it comes to difficult people in our lives.

If indeed we want something (or someone) to change, we must be clear about our intentions, motivation, and goals. How do we find that level of understanding in our lives? In addition to being the author of more than 70 books, Steve Arterburn is also the founder and chairman of New Life Ministries—the nation's largest faith-based broadcast, counseling, and treatment ministry—and host of the nationally syndicated *New Life Live* daily radio program. I particularly love the way Steve addresses this question.

> The bottom line is that relationships are like drinking water: the clearer, the better.
>
> And being clear about who you are and what you want is where being a Christian really comes in handy. Because a dependable and utterly miraculous fact is that praying to Jesus for clarity actually brings clarity.
>
> It's just…unbelievable.
>
> But like so much of the unbelievable stuff God does every second of every day, it's also as true as true gets.

So (and if it sounds like this is our answer to way too many things, it's only because it *is* the answer for just about everything): pray.

If you're in a bad relationship, bring it before Jesus and ask Him to put into your heart and mind what you should do about it. Don't anticipate God's answer to your plea; don't refute His answer; don't give up on Him giving you an answer if within seconds of asking He doesn't give you a Ten-Point Relationship Solving Plan that you can begin executing right away. Just remain faithful, and keep praying.

Trust that when asking for God's help, before long you will get that help. You'll know what to do. You'll know what to say. You'll know how to behave.

And then, of course, you'll have to actually do the things God has shown you to do. That's the other tricky part about being a Christian. We often hear, "Everyone who asks receives" (Luke 11:10). What we hear less often is "Don't ask if you don't want to receive."[1]

Founder of OnCall Prayer and author of the popular *OnCall Prayer Journal*, Sharon Hill has a heart to teach others how to pray and rely on God for every circumstance in their lives. I asked her to share some thoughts on the power of prayer and to give us advice as we navigate the journey of setting boundaries.

It has been my experience that developing a purpose-filled and intentional lifestyle of prayer enhances a Christian walk. It instills a discipline that increases wisdom and moves us from our own strength to God's strength, especially when it comes to dealing with difficult people. But the key word is *intentional*. There is no substitute for prayer, but being consistent in prayer is one of the hardest challenges in my life.

Maybe like me, you have prayed for someone or something for many years. Does God hear your prayers? Does He answer them? In setting healthy boundaries with loved ones for whom I pray and placing them in the hands of God, I am encouraged that no prayer is ever prayed in vain! In Revelation 5:8 we read that our prayers are in golden vials forever active in God's throne room.

I was amazed to learn that Abraham and Sarah waited 30 years after they received the promise that they would bear a son. In Genesis 21:2 we read "Sarah became pregnant and bore a son to Abraham in his old age, at the very time God had promised him."

Delay is not denial.

Did you know that when you write down your thoughts and feelings, it takes them from your subconscious to your conscious mind and gets them down on paper so you can go on with living? I believe journaling is a great release of emotions, an effective cleansing process, a means to hear from God... on paper.

Spending time with God will change your life.

Every decision in life should be made prayerfully, particularly those affecting other people. As you grow in faith and conviction, chances are you'll eventually need to have a conversation with your difficult person. When that time comes, make certain your decision is measured by God's standards. We find out what pleases the Lord by praying, asking, receiving, and reading God's truth in the Word. "Therefore do not be foolish, but understand what the Lord's will is" (Ephesians 5:17).

We've talked about what boundaries are and are not, the core challenges many of us face, and the role of our emotions and temperament in challenging relationships.

To communicate in a healthy way, we need boundaries, and boundaries vary according to the roles we play in a relationship. This comes back to what I said earlier about so many of us being confused about what is and isn't our responsibility. Many of us are unsure of our roles.

Remember, the issue at hand isn't to fix or rescue the difficult person in your life; it's to address the part you play in the relationship that may be contributing to the difficult outcome and to respond in a loving manner while establishing a healthy boundary.

Making Right Decisions

Earlier in this book I shared Dr. Laura's advice about dealing with people who we feel have caused us harm. She said if we want to move forward and grow, we have two options: to stand up or to move on.

Remember, the decision to move on in a relationship doesn't necessarily mean you're giving up or giving in, although that can be the case. Nor does the decision to stand up require you to issue an ultimatum, although that can be the case as well. Either stance can represent forward motion, or personal growth.

Do you want to grow in a relationship that has been weighed down in pain and stress? If so, ask God for help. Confess to God that you are at the end of your resources and that you need Him to guide you to either stand up or move on. And should the time come when you are led to have that conversation with the difficult person in your life, ask God to help you speak the truth in love. "Speaking the truth in love, we will grow to become in every respect the mature body of him who is the head, that is, Christ" (Ephesians 4:15).

In part 2, we'll talk about the Six Steps to SANITY—the tools we need to begin living the hopeful life God intends for us to live.

SANITY Support

1. This chapter challenges us to place the difficult relationship we are in into God's hands. The obvious question is, have you done that? And the next question is, have you left it in God's hands, or do you keep taking it back? If you have difficulty leaving it in His hands, examine your struggle with God. What keeps you from leaving it with Him? What are you afraid of? Or is it that you don't like His answer?

2. Read Ephesians 4:15 again. How would you speak to the difficult person in your life if you spoke the truth in love?

3. Write down what you think about this statement from

this chapter: "The issue at hand isn't to fix or rescue the difficult person in your life; it's to address the part you play in the relationship that may be contributing to the difficult outcome and to respond in a loving manner while establishing a healthy boundary."

Part 2

…Get Set…

10

The Power of SANITY

To see my spice cupboard, you would think I must be quite the culinary wizard. I do enjoy cooking, but truth be told, I'm not very good at it. Nonetheless, sometimes I'll pore over cooking magazines, certain I'll be able to re-create a delectable dish in a photograph. To that end, over the years I've amassed a collection of spices from A to Z that would impress even the most creative chef.

Recently, I came across recipe for a rather elaborate dish. The photograph made my mouth water, and perusing the ingredients added to my anticipation—I realized I already had everything, including a few rather obscure spices, so a special trip to the grocery store would not be necessary.

I rolled up my sleeves and set to work, feeling every bit like Rachael Ray or Martha Stewart, maneuvering around my kitchen like a skater in a rink (albeit a very small rink).

After literally hours of preparation it was time to taste my masterpiece.

The flavor of the dish was indescribable—indescribably *bland*. It was virtually void of flavor. *How could this be?*

I was certain I'd followed the instructions to a *T*. Yet after careful observation I made a startling discovery: Spices have expiration dates. Who knew?

It turned out that most of the pretty jars in my spice cupboard contained nothing but worthless powders and useless herbs. Any flavor they may have once held was long gone. Lacking value and effectiveness, my only recourse was to throw them out.

Throwing things away is really hard for some of us, whether they are tangible items, bad habits, or unhealthy behaviors. We often hang on to things that no longer serve useful purposes and that may even keep us from being all God wants us to be and from God Himself.

> You are the salt of the earth. But if the salt loses its saltiness, how can it be made salty again? It is no longer good for anything, except to be thrown out and trampled underfoot.
>
> You are the light of the world. A town built on a hill cannot be hidden. Neither do people light a lamp and put it under a bowl. Instead they put it on its stand, and it gives light to everyone in the house. In the same way, let your light shine before others, that they may see your good deeds and glorify your Father in heaven (Matthew 5:13-16).

The old spices we keep using are no longer working. They lack flavor and effectiveness. As we become more sensitive to interactions that cross our boundaries, we need to replace our usual responses with new salt. We need to let our light shine.

Moving Forward

We now know establishing boundaries is essential to creating and maintaining mental, physical, emotional, and spiritual health.

Some of us have suffered severe violations to our boundaries, and gaining clarity and balance might require the additional help of a trained professional. Others of us might simply need to be aware of the emotional triggers that set us off and learn to head them off at the pass, or to better understand the strengths and weaknesses of our natural-born temperaments and how to accentuate the positives and temper the negatives.

Either way, the Six Steps to SANITY can provide a powerful prescription for a host of boundary-setting challenges, a type of all-purpose medication to help us find hope and healing regardless of what we are facing.

SANITY is a way back to God.

So What Exactly Is SANITY?

SANITY is what we gain when we shift our priorities and stop focusing on difficult people, the problems of others, and the situations and circumstances of life, and begin to focus on changing our own attitudes and behaviors—starting with our hearts. As God makes a difference in us, we can make a difference in others.

Remember this key Scripture: "Above all else, guard your heart, for everything you do flows from it" (Proverbs 4:23).

Our ultimate goal in achieving SANITY is to guard our hearts and to enjoy right relationships with God and with others in our lives. It's to gain the necessary wisdom to make rational and godly choices in all areas of our lives and to set healthy boundaries so we can truly help ourselves, our families, and others in authentic and loving ways.

God did not mean for us to suffer through tumultuous relationships. He has a far greater purpose for us and for those we are in relationship with.

In the original manuscript of my first book, *God Allows U-Turns*, I recounted my life story. I based my story on 2 Corinthians 5:17: "Therefore, if anyone is in Christ, the new creation has come. The old has gone, the new is here!"

God Allows U-Turns was never published as the memoir it was originally intended to be, but instead as a collection of true short stories from many different writers that illustrate the timeless truth that we can never be so lost or so broken that we cannot turn around and head back to God. The *U-Turns* message was all about changed lives, which is really all about our willingness to acknowledge God and let Him change our lives.

In his book *The Hole in Our Gospel*, Richard Stearns elicits a call to action that could change the world.

> You and I are not meant to act like preresurrection disciples, racked with fear, doubt and timidity. We are *postresurrection*

disciples, and if we are to live as postresurrection disciples, everything in our lives must change. The question for us is whether we are willing to make that commitment—to live and act differently, and to repair the hole in our own gospel. If we are, then God will use us as parts of His amazing plan to change our world. But becoming this kind of disciple, one who is determined to *be* the gospel to the world around him, involves an intentional decision. It doesn't just happen...We won't really become change agents for Christ just by going to church every Sunday. We will have to make some "on purpose" life choices and then change our priorities and behavior. Only then can God transform us and use us to change the world.[1]

If a challenging relationship with a difficult person has left you broken or is consuming far more time, energy, and resources than you have, it's time to hand it over to God. This isn't just about setting healthy boundaries with difficult people. It's about intentionally giving up the insanity that has consumed many of our earthly relationships and purposefully turning to a relationship with the Lord, where we will always feel loved, cherished, supported, and significant.

It's time for healing—mentally, physically, and spiritually.

It's time to find SANITY!

Six Steps to SANITY

S — *Stop* your own destructive behaviors

A — *Assemble* a support group

N — *Nip* excuses in the bud

I — *Implement* rules and boundaries

T — *Trust* your instincts

Y — *Yield* everything to God (let go and let God)

11

S—*Stop* Your Own Negative Behavior and Destructive Patterns

The first step in any journey of growth may be the hardest, but unless we take that crucial first step, we'll never arrive at our destination. Author June Hunt writes, "When your mind is mired in the mud, you can't move forward, you can't move backward. You're bogged down in the ditch and see no way out, with no one to help."

This first step in the Six Steps to SANITY can bring us illumination and empower us to see more clearly than we have for years—in *all* of our relationships.

Remember the oft-quoted definition of insanity: repeating the same behavior and expecting different results. It's time to stop repeating the negative behaviors and destructive patterns that have not produced the desired results.

If a challenging relationship with an adult child, aging parent, or difficult person has begun to consume your peace and joy, if your life has become increasingly chaotic and painful, it's okay to say, "This is enough." It's okay to stop and step back to gain a better perspective on the situation.

Based on my experience and from feedback I've received from psychologists and counselors, we must take four critical Stop Steps to end the insanity that causes stress and self-destruction—steps that will help us turn our lives around. Accomplishing these four Stop Steps can be life changing.

1. Stop Repeating Your Own Negative Behavior

Talk is cheap.

It's one thing to say we'll stop enabling our adult children, stop allowing toxic parents to infect our lives, stop being the target of rude and disrespectful conduct for a coworker, or stop treating our own needs as though they didn't matter. It's another thing entirely to commit to change and do the necessary work to embark on a journey of self-discovery and self-respect.

Implementing the Six Steps to SANITY requires that we make decisions with a great deal of thought and prayer. We must be ready, willing, and able to give the process of change our total commitment, and we must be fully convinced we need to stop repeating our own negative behaviors. We'll stand strong only if we thoroughly think through and fully commit to our initial commitment to *stop*.

In her book *The Emotionally Destructive Relationship*, Leslie Vernick addressed the truth about change and how it begins when we stop.

> The most painful step in any healing process is often the first one. You must face the ugly truth that you're in a destructive relationship and that you are the one who has allowed it to continue. Just like a person wouldn't begin chemotherapy unless she first accepts that she has cancer, you will not take the steps necessary to grow, heal, or change if you are still in denial. As long as you minimize the truth about your problem, you cannot become strong enough to challenge or change anything. Wherever you are, it is important you realize that stopping the destructive dance starts with you.[1]

The change starts with us.

Therefore, stop repeating your own negative behavior.

"All who are prudent act with knowledge, but fools expose their folly" (Proverbs 13:16).

2. Stop Ignoring Your Own Personal Issues

Boundaries come in all shapes and sizes. They can be intrusive, distant, or safe and loving.

When we grow up in dysfunctional families, talking about healthy boundaries can be like trying to speak a foreign language—we may have no idea what's being said. By the time we reach adulthood, many of us have acquired reasonably acceptable coping mechanisms to get by.

Yet is "just getting by" all we aspire to? Doesn't God want (and promise) so much more than that?

Years ago, after decades of just getting by, I checked myself into a one-month treatment program to sort out the mess I had made of my own life. Only then did I begin to see my negative behaviors and destructive patterns (especially the enabling component) for what they were. I wrote about this in *Setting Boundaries with Your Adult Children*.

> There are so many extenuating circumstances as to why we do the things we do, and so many intricate components to how we've arrived at this place in life. However, in my experience there appears to be a common theme in the overall pathology of enabling parents—and that theme is the general neglect of our own hearts. Whether it's a relatively minor issue that needs to be addressed or a major malady, the fact tends to be global that in focusing so much time and energy on the problems of our adult children, we have neglected the issues that have made us who we are today. We must be willing to look inwardly at ourselves to identify our reasons for allowing things to get so out of hand. We cannot begin to implement the changes that need to occur if we aren't willing to recognize the part we play in the drama.[2]

Do you need to acknowledge any personal issues, regardless of whether they directly concern your difficult person? Think about it. Pray about it. What must you deal with in your own life at this time? Whatever the trial, rest assured that God will not give you more than you can handle. This is not merely a Christian platitude—it is God's truth.

Stop ignoring your own personal issues.

"Blessed is the one who perseveres under trial because, having stood the test, that person will receive the crown of life that the Lord has promised to those who love him" (James 1:12).

3. Stop Being Alone in Your Pain

During my season as a new believer, I isolated my situation with my son from others. I believed (wrongly) that good Christians didn't have children who were involved in drugs, crime, and a host of other behaviors that make parents' lives chaotic, crazy, insane. In time, I came to understand that was not the case, as I wrote in *Setting Boundaries with Your Adult Children*.

> For too long we've felt like outcasts in a world of perfect parents and perfect kids, when in reality there are families just like ours all around us. Parents in pain exist in our church home, in our workplace, and in our neighborhood—often suffering in silence. Support groups such as Al-Anon and Co-Dependents Anonymous meet in locations around the country. Joining, or in some cases starting, a support group is vital. Professional therapy is often the best way to go when we need to make significant changes in our lives. Having the benefit of an objective opinion and the therapeutic advice of a professional is invaluable. In addition to professional counseling on an hourly or sliding-scale basis, many resources are available to us at little or no cost. We may have to do a bit of research to find them, but it will be worth it. For many of us, it's much too difficult to heal without objective, qualified, and nonjudgmental help.[3]

It's important to not isolate yourself during this time of change, regardless of what you may be dealing with. We were created to be in relationship—with God the Father and with other brothers and sisters in Christ. Additionally, there is nothing to be ashamed of if you feel the need to talk with a professional counselor or psychologist to get your life back on track—in fact, it could be the best call you ever make.

Therefore, stop being alone in your pain.

"I tell you that if two of you on earth agree about anything they ask for, it will be done for them by my Father in heaven. For where two or three gather in my name, there am I with them" (Matthew 18:19-20).

4. Stop Pushing God out of the Picture

Turning (or returning) to our faith during times of trial and tribulation is not unusual. God will often use the most painful experiences to teach us the most profound lessons. But God is so much more than a lifeguard who is standing by, ready to rescue us when we're drowning.

God created us for a love relationship with Him. He wants to be involved in every area of our lives. Unfortunately, we often assign God a limited place in our lives. What kind of love relationship is that?

"Hear, O Israel: The LORD our God, the LORD is one. Love the LORD your God with all your heart and with all your soul and with all your strength" (Deuteronomy 6:4-5).

To be loved by God is the highest relationship possible, the highest achievement, and the highest position in life. Our relationship to God (Father, Son, and Spirit) is the single most important aspect of our lives. We talked about this at some length in an earlier chapter—our need to embrace the most important relationship. God wants us to love Him with our total being. He created us for that very purpose. If our relationship with Him is out of line, everything else related to knowing, doing, and experiencing God's will is going to be out of balance and messed up as well.

This was certainly the case when I was so entrenched in enabling my adult son, as well as recently during the challenging relationship with my family member that I discussed earlier. The messier the situation got, the less one-on-one time I spent with God. Not because I didn't trust Him—that was never the case. It was because the increasing problems (many of them boundary-related) I was having with this difficult person began to consume me, robbing me of peace, joy, time, sleep, and eventually my health. I was so weary I couldn't see straight.

Thankfully, through the loving-kindness and prayers of close friends who helped me to reach the place where I could stand up and say,

"Enough is enough," I began the journey back to restoring the most important relationship in my life.

I love what Henry Blackaby writes about this in his acclaimed book *Experiencing God.*

> When your life is in the middle of God's activity, He will start rearranging a lot of your thinking. God's ways and thoughts are so different from yours and mine that they will often sound wrong, crazy, or impossible. Often, you will realize that the task is far beyond your power or resources to accomplish. When you recognize that the task is humanly impossible, you need to be ready to believe God and trust Him completely.
>
> You need to believe that He will enable and equip you to do everything He asks of you. Don't try to second-guess Him. Just let Him be God. Turn to Him for the needed power, insight, skill, and resources. He will provide you with all you need.[4]

Difficult people are never going to go away—at least not in this lifetime. That's why learning how to be in reasonably healthy relationships with them begins by learning how to be in a relationship with the One who loves you the most.

Therefore, stop pushing God out of the picture.

When We Stop, the Healing Starts

The *S* step in SANITY will set the course for all of the steps that follow. Once we finally own up to our negative behavior for what it is—and how damaging it's become—we will be much less likely to continue the same behavior while expecting different results. God willing, we will feel a deep conviction in our souls to make choices that will change our lives.

When we finally stop and say, "Enough is enough," God often makes Himself known in miraculous ways.

"Come to me, all you who are weary and burdened, and I will give you rest" (Matthew 11:28).

SANITY Support

1. Taking ownership of our negative behaviors is never easy. We excuse our negative behaviors by not taking into account the harmful impact they have on others. What negative behaviors do you need to honestly and courageously take responsibility for?

2. One of the biggest problems we face as human beings trying to relate well to other human beings is that we tend to transfer our personal issues onto the other people we are trying to relate to. Are there any unresolved personal issues that you tend to transfer onto other people? If so, name those issues.

3. How are you coping with the pain of your difficult relationship? Are you isolating yourself, or are you seeking out others to share your feelings with? If you are not seeking out others to help you, what is it that is keeping you from doing that? Whom could you share with? Make a commitment to share your painful relationship with a trusted friend or to find a caring counselor.

4. God's goal for you in this life is that you become conformed into the image of His Son, Jesus (Romans 8:28-29). He will use whatever means necessary to accomplish that goal, even the pain of difficult relationships. How can knowing this help you to walk more closely with God during this difficult time?

As a reminder of the things you need to stop, photocopy the list on the next page and put it in a place where you'll see it often—the refrigerator door, a bulletin board, a bedroom mirror, or some other prominent place.

STEP 1 TO SANITY: I WILL...

Stop repeating the same responses and expecting different results.

Stop my own negative behavior and destructive patterns.

Stop ignoring my own personal issues.

Stop being alone in my pain.

Stop pretending things are going to be fine if I continue as I have been.

Stop putting off the changes that must be made.

Stop feeling guilty for past mistakes and choices.

Stop demanding that other people change.

Stop making excuses for other people's negative behavior and choices of others.

Stop engaging in arguments, debates, or negotiations.

12

A—*Assemble* a Support Group

When our 12-week divorce-care support group ended, I came away with an unexpected and deeply appreciated gift from God—the gift of kindred-spirit friendship. Nancy and I had clicked from the start, and our lives became inextricably woven together with threads of shared experience. I was reeling from a very recent and unwanted divorce after almost 14 years of marriage, and after a year, Nancy was still trying to make sense of the end of her 24-year marriage.

Likewise, the relationships that developed when I attended Mercy Heart, an organization dedicated to ministering to the hearts of inmates and their families, have become life-saving gifts from God as I've traveled the journey of my adult son's incarceration and release. The official mission of Mercy Heart is "to assist families and inmates through and beyond transition." (To find out more about Mercy Heart, visit their website at www.MercyHeart.org.) My son has also found deep connections at Mercy Heart weekly support group meetings and at other issue-related support groups he attends regularly, such as Narcotics Anonymous and Celebrate Recovery.

Throughout the years, some of my closest friendships have developed from support-group settings. I have a far deeper connection with those who have sat in the boat with me, frantically bailing water to stay alive, than with those who stand on the shore, regardless of how encouraging they may be.

When our lives on this vast planet intersect, especially during times of intense personal change, these friendships can be profound gifts from God. Miraculous things can and often do happen when we sojourn together as a group to overcome life's obstacles. This includes learning a new pattern of behavior, especially when that new behavior helps us to grow in our walk as Christians.

Two great places to assemble a support group are in church and in an issue-related environment.

Assemble in Church

The Bible teaches that the primary reason for believers to gather is to encourage one another, which gives every follower of Christ the job of being an encourager as well. This fellowship of giving and receiving is vital. Fellowship is not just camaraderie; it is what two or more people experience when they have the same goals and desires, when they think alike and communicate in such a way as to actually enter into the other's experience.

To understand the core of *who* we are requires that we first understand *whose* we are. Therefore, it's important to return to a biblical definition of what it means to be created in God's image. When it comes to our roles as children of the Almighty, men and women are created equally in the image of God.

> God created mankind in his own image, in the image of God he created them; male and female he created them (Genesis 1:27).

> There is neither Jew nor Gentile, neither slave nor free, nor is there male and female, for you are all one in Christ Jesus (Galatians 3:28).

We need only to look in the mirror to see the fingerprint of God's creation. We are worthy and valuable—created in His image! A good way to always remember this vital truth and grow spiritually is to be around like-minded individuals, such as the people in church.

People attend church for many reasons, some merely out of habit or tradition. But church is an opportunity to connect with others of a similar belief and worldview, to remember what Jesus has done for us, and to express joy and thankfulness to God through singing, praying, and hearing God's Word. It's an opportunity (and a blessing!) to come away from the work and pressure of everyday life for spiritual refreshment and fellowship. (Of course, things aren't always rosy in church, but that too can be an opportunity for growth.)

If we've had challenges in setting boundaries, we need to grow as individuals to learn how to break the cycle. The fellowship of the church and the information we receive there are a few of the many tools God uses to grow us as individuals. Some churches fail miserably at this, but many thousands of churches are doing a great job. If you've had a bad experience with church in the past, God does not want you to throw out the baby with the bathwater and stop attending. We shouldn't judge all churches by what some churches do, any more than we should judge all people of one race or religion or institution by what a few members do.

Satan wants to divide and conquer, but God wants to repair the broken pieces and put us together. Gathering together in church is not being Christian—it's simply meeting with people who are collectively worshipping as one body of believers. Rosemary Jensen writes this in the *NIV Women's Devotional Bible*:

> In Scripture, John wanted this kind of communication with his friends. It was as if he was saying to them, "Let me tell you what I have seen and heard of Jesus Christ so that we may have the same mind about Him, the same desire to know Him better, the same experience of Him." Then he goes on to say that we will have this fellowship because we have fellowship with the same Father and the same Son, Jesus Christ. We fellowship with God (the Father and the Son), and He brings us into fellowship with each other. He is the basis for our fellowship because together we share His life.[1]

"We proclaim to you what we have seen and heard, so that you also may have fellowship with us. And our fellowship is with the Father and with his Son, Jesus Christ. We write this to make our joy complete" (1 John 1:3-4).

To help make our joy complete, one of the first support groups we need to assemble in our lives is our church family. Seek out a church in your community; ask family and friends where they attend. Read the colorful glossy postcard invitations that some churches send in the mail. Pray for the Spirit to lead you as you go—but by all means, go. Get connected. It's important.

One more thing before we leave the topic of attending church. The most important thing about your fellowship with other believers is not the denomination (Baptist, Lutheran, Presbyterian, and the like). However, it's good to know what belief system the group is following when you attend any corporate worship. You can usually find this out by reading the statement of faith the church might provide or by visiting their website if they have one. Be wary of any body of believers whose leader or members are unable to provide a written statement of what they believe.

Assemble in an Issue-Related Environment

Assembling in a church environment is important, and assembling with people who are meeting collectively to conquer personal strongholds and gain strength is too. In this setting, you may discover other issues in your life that are contributing to the challenges you are having with difficult people (or they might be having with you).

Anytime we're embarking on a journey of significant personal change and growth, we can greatly benefit from the support, understanding, encouragement, and accountability of others who have traveled the same journey and come out on the other side—or those who are currently walking a similar path and trying to find their way.

In addition to the situation with your difficult person, perhaps you are also dealing with other issues that contribute to the stress in your life. These may include divorce, single parenting, unemployment, financial problems, health concerns, aging parents, or depression, just to name a few. Support groups addressing these topics are undoubtedly meeting somewhere nearby. Gone are the days when attending a support group was considered a sign of weakness, when silent shame and guilt accompanied members into each session.

Traditionally, when we think of support groups, we think of well-known groups such as Alcoholics Anonymous, Celebrate Recovery, or other 12-step groups. AA works because one alcoholic helps another. Today, support groups come in all sizes and varieties. They no longer center on substance abuse alone, which at first was the norm. The following list only scratches the surface of topics that support groups address today.

AIDS, cancer, and other illnesses	incarceration
Alzheimer's	infertility
anger management	marriage enrichment
anxiety	parenting
depression	physical fitness
disabilities	pornography and sexual addiction
divorce	sleep disorders
eating disorders	substance addiction
financial issues	suicide issues
gambling	terminal illness
gay and lesbian issues	unemployment
grief	weight loss

Nowhere in Scripture is the importance of traveling the road together more beautifully depicted than in Ecclesiastes 4:9-12.

> Two are better than one, because they have a good return for their labor: If either of them falls down, one can help the other up. But pity anyone who falls and has no one to help them up. Also, if two lie down together, they will keep warm. But how can one keep warm alone? Though one may be overpowered,

two can defend themselves. A cord of three strands is not quickly broken.

Kent Nowlan knows firsthand the value of assembling in a support group environment. In fact, it saved his life.

> In Narcotics Anonymous we understand that our spiritual condition is the basis of our recovery. God lead me to NA, and NA led me to God. God saved my life, and He used this support group as the tool to do it. The message of hope and the promise of freedom from an active addiction kept me going back week after week and year after year. For an addict, if we use, we lose—it's that simple. We must chase our recovery like we chased our dope. An addict alone is a recipe for disaster, but the fellowship of others to hold us up and hold us accountable is lifesaving.

Support Group Options

It doesn't matter which type of support group you become involved with. It only matters that you get involved. Listening to others share their perspective and their pain allows us to gain objectivity—something many of us lack. Being able to "let it all hang out" in a safe and nonjudgmental environment can be healing and empowering. When it comes to support groups, it's helpful to understand the options available.

Self-help Support Groups

These are organized and managed completely by members, usually volunteers. Alcoholics Anonymous (AA), Narcotics Anonymous (NA), Codependents Anonymous (CoDA), Celebrate Recovery, and Six-Step SANITY Support Groups are examples of self-help groups. They are also sometimes referred to as fellowships, peer support groups, mutual help groups, or mutual aid self-help groups.

Professionally Run Support Groups

These are facilitated by professionals, such as a social worker, a psychologist, or a member of the clergy. The facilitator controls discussions and provides other managerial services. Such professionally run groups are common in institutional settings, such as hospitals, drug treatment centers, and correctional facilities. There may or may not be a fee involved in this type of group.

Online Support Groups

These have been around since at least 1982. Support groups have long offered companionship and information for people coping with diseases or disabilities, but online groups have expanded to offer support for people facing various life circumstances, especially those involving personal and cultural relationships. Diverse remote networking formats have allowed the development of both synchronous groups, where individuals can exchange messages in real time, and asynchronous groups, where members who are not connected to a network at the same time can read and exchange messages. E-mail, Usenet, Internet bulletin boards, chat rooms, and blogs have become popular methods of communication among self-help groups and facilitated support groups.

It's not difficult to find an online support group, but it may be hard to find the right one.

Six-Step SANITY Support Groups

The SANITY Support Groups launched in 2008 in homes, churches, businesses, and community centers. Based on *Setting Boundaries with Your Adult Children*, our first 12-week program met with great success across the USA and in New Zealand, South Africa, Canada, Japan, England, and Germany. Hundreds of parents and grandparents have found hope and healing from the crippling epidemic of enabling adult children.

As word spread and groups were formed around the country, both live and online, it was soon clear the Six Steps to SANITY were applicable to far more issues than just learning how not to enable adult children.

Setting healthy boundaries isn't just a prodigal-child issue.

My prayer has always been that I could offer support to men and women addressing the myriad issues that swirl around the central core of unhealthy boundaries, such as adult children, aging parents, difficult people, teens, food, and other topics.

Therefore, we'll soon be launching new SANITY Support Group programs and services, designed to equip you with the tools you need to live a life of freedom—to experience the hope and healing that comes from clearly defining where you stop and others begin.

To find out if a SANITY Support Group is meeting in your neighborhood, or for guidelines how to begin your own SANITY Support Group, visit our website at SettingBoundariesBooks.com.

Assemble Support Today

As we embark on setting healthy boundaries and making positive changes, we are in a season of life that will most certainly require every ounce of love and fortitude we can muster. We will grow spiritually as individuals through prayer, Bible study, and group praise and worship, as found in church. Additionally, at times when our strength runs low, we will grow as we are able to lean on others who are willing to intervene on our behalf and hold us up, as in a support group environment. We must begin looking at our circumstances objectively, emotionally distancing ourselves from our situations in order to gain a healthy perspective. Making clear choices based on facts and not on feelings will be critical as we move ahead.

Get connected soon in a SANITY Support Group or another reputable organization. Conduct an online search and check with area churches, community centers, nonprofit organizations, friends, and family. Regardless of what you're experiencing, you're not alone. Reach out today.

SANITY Support

1. As you think about assembling a support group, what do you find yourself thinking and feeling? Are you hesitant? Afraid? Are you relieved? Excited? Explore your thoughts

and feelings about this step and write about them in your journal.

2. Unless we set a goal and formulate a plan on how to achieve that goal, most of us will never move toward change. Write out your goal of joining a support group and the steps you will take to make that goal a reality.

3. Whom can you invite to come to a support group with you? Chances are, some of your friends or family could benefit from the support of a group.

13

N—*Nip* Excuses in the Bud

In his book *Dealing with the CrazyMakers in Your Life,* Dr. David Hawkins recounts a story about the time he and his wife were at JFK airport in New York, returning from a peaceful vacation. They had just just spent two weeks in a Spanish resort town on the Mediterranean, and the airport's assault on their senses was a wake-up call.

"Our chaos detectors blared their alarm: *Too much. Can't take it. Sensory overload. Danger. Get out now.*"[1]

After taking time off, he and his wife were now attuned to the fact that what they were experiencing at the airport wasn't a rational way to live. The incredible din, sardine-like cramming of bodies, people rushing and arguing, and babies crying were too much at one time. This was not how God intended anyone to live.

Dr. Hawkins explains in more detail many of the situations we experience when we must deal with crazy-making situations and personalities, and how we've come to accept this out-of-control life as something over which we have no control. We've been living this way for so long, we don't understand how wrong this is.

Could it be that the warning lights alerting us to something wrong in our lives are no longer working? That we've been ignoring boundaries and accepting excuses for so long that our chaos detectors are broken?

When we make the decision to resign from whatever role we're playing in our difficult people's dramas, the story line can quickly turn even more melodramatic. When we decide to set boundaries and find balance, the excuses for why we shouldn't follow through can pop up like weeds in a garden. For example…

- My brother made some bad spending choices again this past month, but he's promised to do better. I'm just going to help him out a little one more time.

- My husband had a really bad childhood, and that's why he…

- I told my neighbor she can't drop by every day to visit, but I feel bad when she…

- My dad has had a rough year. He didn't mean to hit my mom; it was an accident.

- Mom never had much when she was a kid, so I can't fault her for wanting a few nice things. She doesn't mean to overspend.

- My boss is under a lot of stress. She doesn't mean to yell.

Can you think of any excuses that frequently come into play in your relationships with difficult people? If so, write them in your notebook now. Use a fresh page and write this at the top: Excuses to Nip in the Bud.

Another excuse often keeps us from finding freedom in challenging relationships and from nurturing our most important relationship. It sounds like this: "God understands how busy I am, so surely He doesn't expect me to read my Bible and have a quiet time every day."

I came to know the Lord as an adult. I was 35. As a new believer, I treasured Bible study and looked forward to it daily. When I first discovered the wisdom contained in the Word, I was hooked. My initial hunger for knowledge was so visceral that I assumed spiritual discipline was automatically acquired through salvation. Both were new to me, transforming my life in ways I'd never imagined possible.

My hunger and thirst to know God has never dissipated, but I have sometimes let busyness take over my life, robbing me of quiet devotional time and keeping me from making God's Word a priority. Drs. Cloud and Townsend address this problem.

> When some people read the Bible, they see a book of rules, dos and don'ts. When others read it, they see a philosophy of life, principles for the wise. Still others see mythology, stories about the nature of human existence and the human dilemma.
>
> Certainly, the Bible contains rules, principles, and stories that explain what it is like to exist on this Earth. But to us, the Bible is a living book about relationship. Relationship of God to people, people to God, and people to each other. It is about the God who created this world, placed people in it, related to people, lost their relationship, and continues to heal that relationship. It is about God as creator: This is his creation. It is about God as a ruler: He ultimately controls his world and will govern it. And it is about God as redeemer: He finds, saves, and heals his loved ones who are lost and in bondage.[2]

Setting boundaries is all about healing the relationships in our lives. To do that, we need to learn new behaviors and new standards by which to live. We need to nip excuses in the bud—excuses that justify negative behavior as well as excuses that keep us from walking in right priority. And the only way we are going to understand what is a right priority is to spend time with the Author of priorities—God.

Something happens inside us when we read and study the Word. The Lord quickens our hearts and changes us. He brings us wisdom, discernment, and strength. It's not enough to just read Scripture once in a while, see it on a wall hanging, or read it on a bracelet. Reading the Word daily is as life-giving as ingesting food and water. It's all about learning, growing, and making changes according to God's Word and the way He works on us and in us.

What we know today will change, including our feelings, thoughts, perspectives, and knowledge. What will not change is the Word of God.

"As for God, his way is perfect: The LORD's word is flawless; he shields all who take refuge in him" (2 Samuel 22:31).

Jennifer Kennedy Dean is the founder of the Praying Life Foundation and the national prayer director for the Christian Women in Media Association. Her "Word of the Week" encouragement recently addressed this same topic. "To live in intimacy with God, we must build into our lives the disciplines of solitude and silence. We must respond when the Lover of our souls calls us to a place of solitude to be alone with Him."

"Therefore I am now going to allure her; I will lead her into the wilderness and speak tenderly to her" (Hosea 2:14).

The Most Debilitating Excuse

There are many different excuses for living in bondage to poor choices, difficult people, and challenging situations and circumstances. Yet as varied as the excuses are, many begin with the same two words that we need to remove from our vocabulary—*I can't*.

June Hunt is the founder of Hope for the Heart, a worldwide biblical counseling ministry that provides numerous resources for people seeking help. She hosts a live, two-hour call-in counseling program called *Hope in the Night* and is the author of numerous books, including *Counseling Through Your Bible Handbook* and *How to Handle Your Emotions*. In her book *Seeing Yourself Through God's Eyes*, June speaks powerfully to those detrimental words.

> For thousands of years a club has been in existence offering memberships throughout the world. It's a popular club, a prolific club. It's the "I Can't Club."
>
> Under the bylaws, club members are required to make "I can't" statements with conviction: "I can't help but hate him after what he's done to me." "I can't quit this sin." "I can't forgive again!" Such fervor makes it sound as if each "I can't" statement is an unchangeable, universal law.
>
> If you're a member, your pledge echoes the club's premise: No one can win over sin. You believe its promise: defeat is normal. And you promote its purpose: to fill each mind with futility.

One law of science to which everyone is subject is the law of gravity—the force that pulls every object toward the center of earth. Likewise, the members of the "I Can't Club" are prisoners to the downward pull of defeat. They are not only ground-bound, but also sin-bound.

Do you feel bound to a specific sin? Does quitting the "I Can't Club" seem impossible? As a child of God, the word *can't* doesn't have to control your life. Upon your salvation, He gives you the Spirit of God so that you will have the strength of God. He deals a deathblow to the "I Can't Club." He makes it possible for you to overcome any sin. How? By replacing one law for another: "The law of the Spirit of life set me free from the law of sin and death" (Romans 8:2).[3]

When Excuses Stop Working

As you take the Six Steps to SANITY, you'll soon be able to identify excuses quickly—your own as well others'. Once we see an excuse for what it really is—a way to justify our actions or avoid the truth—we can then address the real issue at the heart of the matter.

Pray that God will reveal to your heart the seeds of excuses so you can eradicate them from your life before they germinate and bear bad fruit.

SANITY Support

1. Earlier in this chapter, you were asked to write down the excuses that you give the difficult people in your life for their harmful behavior. Have you done that? If not, write those excuses down in your journal.

2. Read over the list of excuses. Rewrite each one in a way that does not allow you to continue to believe the excuse. For example, if you wrote "My mom was raised in an abusive home; that is why she treats me badly," change

it to this: "My mom was raised in an abusive home, but that does not give her permission to treat me badly."

3. What excuses do you make for your own shortcomings and limitations? Examine them to see if they are true. Rewrite them to fit reality.

14

I—*Implement* Rules and Boundaries

Implementing rules and boundaries is all about taking action. We can talk all we want about finding SANITY, but until we're willing to do the necessary work to change, very little will change.

When we take action, change will most assuredly come one way or another whether we are prepared or not. Whenever possible, I always opt for being prepared.

Part of change is expressing it—declaring it to ourselves and to others. Drs. Cloud and Townsend call this the Law of Exposure.

The Law of Exposure

The whole concept of boundaries has to do with the fact that we exist in relationship. Therefore, boundaries are really about relationship, and finally about love. That's why the Law of Exposure is so important.

The Law of Exposure says that your boundaries need to be made visible to others and communicated to them in relationship. We have many boundary problems because of relational fears. We are beset by fears of guilt, not being liked, loss of love, loss of connection, loss of approval, receiving anger, being known, and so on. These are all failures in love, and God's plan is that we learn how to love. These relational problems can only be solved in relationships, for that is the context of the problems themselves, and the context of spiritual existence.

Because of these fears, we try to have secret boundaries. We withdraw passively and quietly, instead of communicating an honest no to someone we love. We secretly resent instead of telling someone that we are angry about how they have hurt us. Often, we will privately endure the pain of someone's irresponsibility instead of telling them how their behavior affects us and other loved ones, information that would be helpful to their soul.

In other situations, a partner will secretly comply with her spouse, not offering her feelings or opinions for 20 years, and then suddenly "express" her boundaries by filing for divorce. Or parents will "love" their children by giving in over and over for years, not setting limits, and resenting the love they are showing. The children grow up never feeling love because of the lack of honesty, and their parents are befuddled, thinking, "after all we've done."

In these instances, because of unexpressed boundaries, the relationships suffer. An important thing to remember about boundaries is that they exist, and they will affect us, whether or not we communicate them. We suffer when we do not communicate the reality of our boundaries. If our boundaries are not communicated and exposed directly, they will be communicated indirectly or through manipulation.[1]

Put It in Writing

One of the best ways to communicate and directly expose our new boundaries is to put them in writing. First, I recommend you develop a document for your eyes only. At this point, you are communicating only with yourself, so there's no need to filter or censor your words. This is a way to express thoughts and feelings you need to expose regardless of whether you eventually communicate them to the difficult person in your life.

Please do not underestimate the value of this exercise.

"But Allison, I'm not a writer. I'm really not very good at things like this."

Is that an excuse I hear? If so, nip it in the bud!

Define Your Boundary Goals

This written exercise is all about increasing your self-awareness. It's about living an intentional and purposeful life. As you write, pray for the Lord to reveal what you should do concerning the difficult person in your life. You may have discovered by now that the real problem isn't your boss but rather the way you've related to your father; maybe the issue isn't about your nosey neighbor as much as it is the violation of a personal boundary when you were a little girl.

It's never too late to make new personal discoveries that will help you set boundaries and build healthy relationships.

Grab your notebook and write down the seven steps listed below. Under each heading write the first things that come to mind. There is no right or wrong way to do this—just do it.

1. What isn't working?

2. What needs to be done to make it work?

3. What needs to happen first?

4. What will be the consequences?

5. Discuss issues with a support group.

6. Rehearse, practice, and role-play.

7. Begin.

Here's a great way to look at this step. Let's say you have an out-dated kitchen. You know it's not working for you, and so you decide to conduct a major remodeling project. You gather pen and paper, and you start your list.

1. Identify what isn't working.

    Cupboards are too small.

    Dishwasher is broken.

    Not enough counter space.

2. What needs to be done to make it work?

    Replace cupboards and dishwasher.

Build a center island or extend the countertops.

3. What needs to be done first?

    We have five kids—I need my dishwasher!

4. What will be the consequences?

    If we extend the counter, we lose space in dining room.

    Replacing appliances will cost money and eat into our
       savings.

    Our family will be disrupted for weeks, maybe months.

5. Assemble a support group.

    Consult with others who have remodeled.

    Shop around to find out what materials will cost.

    Find out about permits.

    Get bids from contactors.

6. Rehearse and practice.

    Make scale drawings.

    Try building a model.

    Determine how much time each step will take.

7. Begin!

    Hire your crew.

    Set the start and end dates.

Get the picture? Consider your journey to setting healthy boundaries a life-remodeling project! Using the same seven steps, write out your plan. Here's an example:

1. Identify what isn't working.

    My coworker keeps giving me her work to do.

    I'm spending way too many hours at work trying to
       get everything done.

2. What needs to be done to make it work?

> She needs to stop giving me her work to do.
>
> I need to tell her that I cannot do her work.

3. What needs to be done first?

> I need to tell her no the next time she asks.

4. Consider the consequences.

> She might get angry with me.
>
> She may refuse to talk to me.
>
> She could bad-mouth me behind my back.

5. Discuss issues with a support group member.

> If this doesn't stop I could go to our supervisor, but I hate to do that.
>
> I need to get feedback from my support group.

6. Practice.

> "I would really like to help you with that project, but I need to stay on task with my responsibilities. Perhaps you should discuss it with Mr. Hall?"

7. Ready, set, go!

> I commit to making a change in how I respond to my coworker.
>
> I will speak with my coworker on our break.

Do this written exercise as many times as you need to until you have a clear picture of what the issue really is and what needs to happen to make a change.

We've established that to set healthy boundaries, we need to understand our own negative behavior and destructive patterns. This may include learning to say no, to be loving yet tough, and to be self-reliant. Hope lies in learning to depend on God and to make choices that will change our lives and not just perpetuate the status quo. You will enjoy a landmark moment in your life when you can calmly and rationally express your needs, even if you do it on paper.

Considering the Consequences

An important part of implementing rules and boundaries will be the work you do in exploring the natural consequences that may occur as you enforce healthy boundaries. The more prepared you are, the more likely you are to hold firm in your resolve. Curveballs often throw us for a loop. We must have a game plan.

To prepare for possible scenarios, actually write down and rehearse your responses to situations that might arise when you set a boundary. Of course, you can't predict everything, but you know your difficult person, and you most likely know what the hot-button topics will be.

For example, let's say babysitting your grandchildren is the issue. In this hypothetical situation, your son is divorced from the mother of your two small grandchildren. He lives in another state and is not involved in their lives, but his ex-wife lives in your city, and she has allowed you to maintain an active relationship with the children.

However, your ex-daughter-in-law has begun to take advantage of you. She goes out with her friends several times a week and often leaves the grandkids with you overnight. She almost never calls beforehand, but just shows up on your doorstep with the baby in her arms and the toddler standing nearby, clutching a blankie.

As much as you love your grandkids, this is not the season in your life to be practically raising two young children. This pattern must stop. Even if you're going to be home and don't have plans, the next time she shows up at your door unannounced, you could tell her in a calm, even-tempered voice, "You know I love the girls and I want to help when I can, but I'm not able to watch them this evening. I'm sorry, but you'll need to find someone else. And in the future, I really need you to call ahead and ask if I can babysit."

Considering this hypothetical situation, what are the possible consequences to the boundary you have established? List them in your notebook.

Present a Written Plan

In some extreme situations, it may be beneficial to present a written plan of action to the difficult person in your life. Such is often the case with parents who are confronting adult children dealing with addictions or other serious dysfunctional behavior. When parents make their new boundaries visible to their adult children in writing, things really begin to happen. This level of communication has been nonexistent for many of these families. Assumptions and silence are no longer allowed to prevail.

I advocate verbal communication in person whenever possible, but sometimes written communication may be the best alternative for defining a new boundary with a difficult person. To help you construct your letter, we've included sample letters starting on page 223. Written by Bernis Riley, a licensed Christian counselor, these letters, or scripts, will give you a good start in formulating your own words. Bernis made this comment about the advantages of this approach:

> It is often very helpful to write out what you would like to say to a person before you say it. By writing out a letter or a script to your difficult person you accomplish three things:
>
> 1. You get to say what you want to say without interruption.
>
> 2. You get time to think about what you want to say without having to think on your feet.
>
> 3. You can weed out the unnecessary stuff you might want to say but do not need to say.

Setting healthy boundaries allows your true self to emerge. Living an authentic life is something to be relished, and it's never too late to implement rules and boundaries—to make choices that will change your life. Trust that God *can* transform your relationships with your difficult people, just as He has transformed us.

SANITY Support

1. Have you written out new boundaries? If not, follow the seven steps in this chapter for setting new boundaries (or reinforcing old ones) with your difficult person.

2. Do not move on to the next chapter until you have completed the question above.

15

T—*Trust* Your Instincts

It's amazing to me that so many of us make important decisions about life and relationships that are in direct opposition to our gut feelings, or natural instincts. We know what is right, yet we allow ourselves to be controlled by other influences, such as emotions, excuses, or the fear of possible consequences.

Dozens of parents in pain who responded to a questionnaire I formulated for *Setting Boundaries with Your Adult Children* berated themselves for not paying more attention to their instincts. One anonymous mother had a particularly bad experience.

> My son drove a new car and had not one but two fancy motor-cycles. He had a good job selling office equipment, but I knew he wasn't making enough money to afford those things. He had all kinds of reasons for the stuff he brought home: "A friend gave me this cool MP3 player," or "I got a great deal on the cycle; I couldn't pass it up," or "I'm just storing the 42-inch flat-panel TV here until my buddy moves," and on and on the stories went. I was such a sap to believe him, and what makes me even angrier is that I had a feeling something wasn't right. I felt in my gut that something was wrong.
>
> He was arrested for dealing drugs. When the police searched our home, they found a floor safe under the carpet in his room containing cash, jewelry, cocaine, and methamphetamine.

He'd installed a floor safe in our home without our knowledge! It cost us considerable legal fees to clear our own names, as we faced charges of being accessories. Although it was embarrassing to admit that we were duped in such a way, it was more of a nightmare to think we might actually have to suffer the consequences of not following our instincts. Thankfully, we were exonerated, but our son is serving an extended sentence in a federal prison. He has placed our names on the list of visitors he refuses to see.

Did this happen overnight? Did young Johnny wake up one day deciding to deal drugs, using his parents' home as a storehouse for his stash? Highly unlikely.

Likewise, in our own situations, did some of the difficult people in our lives only recently begin treating us so poorly? Or have their toxic behaviors been present for years?

We often know when something in a relationship is wrong—when that inner voice speaks to our hearts about specific situations or issues. Yet we repeatedly ignore the voice and negate the instinct. Intuition is a powerful tool. However, that still small voice will eventually stop talking altogether if we continue to ignore it.

When I was a girl, I loved to watch the TV program *Lost in Space*. The Robinson family had such amazing adventures! For years afterward, anytime I felt in my gut that trouble was imminent, I would hear the warning phrase of the robot echo in my mind: "Danger, Will Robinson, danger! Danger, Will Robinson, danger!" Oh, that we had our own flailing-armed robot to shout words of warning to us concerning our inability to set appropriate boundaries!

Back in my years as a new Christian, I was given a copy of *The Bible Promise Book*, a paperback filled with Scriptures listed under alphabetical categories ranging from "Anger" to "Word of God." I've gone through numerous copies of this powerful little paperback over the years because it leads me to verses based on the issues I'm experiencing. Under the topic "Trust" are multiple verses to study, including Proverbs 3:5-6: "Trust in the LORD with all your heart and lean not on your own understanding; in all your ways acknowledge him, and he will make your paths straight."

Trusting our instincts isn't only knowing when someone is lying, cheating, or breaking the law. It's listening to God speaking to us.

If we trust in the Lord with all our heart, we must also trust what He teaches us about the power of the Holy Spirit.

> I will ask the Father, and he will give you another advocate to help you and be with you forever—the Spirit of truth. The world cannot accept him, because it neither sees him nor knows him. But you know him, for he lives with you and will be in you (John 14:16-17).

There are countless Scripture references on the amazing power of the Holy Spirit. I encourage you to take time to study this powerful aspect of our faith. In my experience, I've found this one thing to be true: When I am walking in God's will for my life, I can clearly feel the power of the Holy Spirit within me, and this often manifests itself in very distinct impressions of how I should respond, behave, and think. It's as though my instinct is a divine power, guiding me to do what is right. This powerful "inside track" of guidance is available to each and every one of us who believes.

Remember the story about "swearing Ted"? As I began to feel assaulted by his words, my emotions kicked in, but this time, so did the still, small voice of the Holy Spirit, telling me I needed to speak up in a firm but loving way. The resulting conversation is one I will long remember, and I hope the same can be said by those who were in attendance that day.

Let me tell you, when the Holy Spirit wins out and we are able to conquer the demons of habitual poor choice responses, it is a victory to be celebrated!

But this kind of listening takes discipline.

Trusting your instincts and not worldly lies, emotional uncertainly, or even the head knowledge you may have becomes more natural as we understand God's truth and hide it in our hearts. We need to have our roots firmly established in God. We need to know the standard God has established for us as His children and the powerful truth contained in His Word so that when the still, small voice of the Holy Spirit speaks to us, we can hear it loud and clear and trust it implicitly.

Trust Your Instincts

Is something telling you not to engage in another argument with your ex-husband? Not to respond in your usual manner to your sister? Is something telling you to reach out and hug your mother-in-law when every fiber of your being wants to turn around and walk away? Can you hear God's Word speaking to your heart, telling you not to lean on your own understanding, but to trust in Him?

Is that still, small voice getting louder?

If so, listen to it. Trust your instincts.

"Blessed is the one who trusts in the LORD, whose confidence is in him" (Jeremiah 17:7).

SANITY Support

1. Whose voice have you been listening to about your relationship with a difficult person? Is it the voice of the enemy, who speaks lies, fear, and discouragement? Or are you listening to the voice of truth, that of the Holy Spirit, who speaks assurance and courage?

2. Trusting God means that you demand nothing. How have you defined what it means to trust God? Write that out in your journal.

3. Is it difficult for you to trust your instincts and to listen to the prompting of the Holy Spirit? If so, why might this might be difficult for you?

16

Y—*Yield* Everything to God

At some point, every Christian adult will have to release his or her problems to God and learn to trust Him for whatever happens.

When I distributed my questionnaire for *Setting Boundaries with Your Adult Children*, virtually every respondent agreed that although each of the Six Steps to SANITY was vital in making transformational life changes, the *Y* step was the most critical. Yet while everyone agreed that it was indeed a vital component, they equally agreed it was one of the most difficult aspects of actively applying faith to our daily walk.

True Growth Requires Letting Go

In addition to being an author, Leslie Vernick is a licensed clinical social worker and the director of Christ-Centered Counseling for Individuals and Families. Day after day, she sees firsthand the devastating effects people's pasts have on their present experience. Underlying virtually every issue is the mistake many of us make in hanging on tightly to the reins of our lives—or the lives of others. Leslie knows that true growth requires letting go. She writes about this in her book *The Emotionally Destructive Relationship*.

> When we attempt to accomplish greater emotional and spiritual work, we usually think about all the things we need to *add* to our lives. We want to read and study the Bible, do meaningful ministry, gain greater emotional stability, better

our interpersonal skills, or seek additional wisdom. All these endeavors can be helpful in our maturing process. But I have found in my own life as well as in my counseling practice that deeper and more lasting change usually comes about when we regularly practice letting go rather than doing more.

Recently I was speaking with Richard, a client who feared God's judgment when he died because he wasn't working harder to do more. As we talked I said, "Perhaps we've gotten the concept of final judgment wrong. What if, in the end, Jesus isn't going to tell us everything we've ever done wrong or failed to do? What if he's going to show us the person we could have become and the things we would have done if only we allowed him to heal and mature us?"[1]

True healing begins when we make the head-heart connection that we must "let go and let God" concerning all things, not just the painful situations that often occur when we have relationships with difficult people. Leslie writes more about this in her book.

Letting go in order to grow can be scary. It requires change, which demands a certain degree of faith and hope. That's why our picture of God must heal, at least a little, before we can embark on greater growth.

The writer of Hebrews reminds us that we can only let go and run the race of life well when we keep our eyes on Jesus. Abiding and surrender…continue to be important as we practice the discipline of letting go.[2]

Leslie says we must learn to let go of three things if we want greater healing and maturity in our lives: unrealistic expectations, negative emotions, and lies.

When we have "let go" in our hearts and are focusing on "letting God," something amazing begins to happen. We feel free. We may not even realize how our fears had bound us until those fears are gone.

You may have heard me on radio or seen me on TV as I talk about my relationship with my adult son—my only child. You know it's still very difficult for me, even after countless interviews and talks, to share parts of the story without emotion and tears. Some aspects of setting boundaries are painful. Sometimes it hurts to do the right thing, just as it sometimes hurts to remember the wrong things we have done or that people have done to us.

I don't know exactly what you are going through right now in your relationships with difficult people. I don't know the level of pain, frustration, or defeat you may feel. But I do know this—until you can yield, until you can open your arms wide and release these people to God, any kind of true healing is virtually impossible.

When I had an almost soul-shattering realization that I had been assuming the role of God in my son's life, my life (and subsequently his) finally began to change.

When I eventually established firm boundaries to no longer accept responsibility for his choices, I knew the consequences could be severe. I was prepared, as much as one can be. I stopped bailing him out of jail. I stopped allowing him to crash at my home when he was evicted from wherever he had been living. He has lived on the streets, in shelters, in cars, at friends' places…wherever he could until eventually he got tired of running from his consequences.

When he turned himself in to the authorities, I clung to the knowledge that even though my son would spend years behind bars, God had a plan for him. I fought feelings of guilt, refusing to let Satan win, knowing that my son was in prison not because I set boundaries, but because of his own actions, his choices.

When I stepped out of the way and yielded him to God, Chris began the journey he needed to walk—the journey I so often delayed because I thought I was helping, because I couldn't nip excuses in the bud, didn't trust my instincts, and wouldn't consistently implement rules and boundaries.

When I was fully able to yield, when I stopped trying to be God in my son's life, he found God.

"The Lord disciplines the one he loves, and he chastens everyone he accepts as his son. Endure hardship as discipline; God is treating you as his children. For what children are not disciplined by their father?" (Hebrews 12:6-7).

Over the past several years, I have watched as God has disciplined my son—His son. I've watched this angry, irresponsible, and fatherless boy become a man who loves the Lord as an obedient son. I've watched as the storms of trial and tribulation have tested his faith. They have been unable to extinguish the light that has been increasing in spite of the bondage of years of addiction and poor choices.

To yield everything to God is *not* to give up. It is not a sign of defeat or weakness, but is in fact quite the opposite.

Today my son is out of prison, and we are working to restore a relationship that has been ravaged by poor choices, addictions, incarceration, and estrangement. What does forgiveness really look like? How do we learn to trust again? How can families heal and build new memories after setting healthy (and sometimes very painful) boundaries? I have a great many questions that I'm expecting God to answer—in His time.

Unfortunately, I've had to ask those painful questions again as I set boundaries with the family member I mentioned earlier. We cannot know God's ultimate plan when we fully yield ourselves, our loved ones, and our difficult people to Him. Yet none of us travel this path alone.

"Come near to God and he will come near to you" (James 4:8).

The tangible result of finding SANITY is finding a new you and a new life.

Will you continue with business as usual, allowing your challenging relationships to control you? Or are you ready to apply these Six Steps to SANITY to make changes that will transform your life?

The choice is yours.

SANITY Support

1. What unrealistic expectations have you not let go of yet?

2. What negative emotions do you need to acknowledge and give up?

3. What lies (or excuses) do you continue to hold on to that are not helping you set the boundaries necessary for healthy relationships?

THE SIX STEPS TO SANITY

S— *Stop* your own negative behaviors and destructive patterns

A— *Assemble* a support group

N— *Nip* excuses in the bud

I — *Implement* rules and boundaries

T— *Trust* your instincts

Y— *Yield* everything to God (let go and let God)

Part 3

…Go!

17

How to Practice SANITY

There you have it, the Six Steps to SANITY:

> **S** — *Stop* your own negative behaviors and destructive patterns
>
> **A** — *Assemble* a support group
>
> **N** — *Nip* excuses in the bud
>
> **I** — *Implement* rules and boundaries
>
> **T** — *Trust* your instincts
>
> **Y** — *Yield* everything to God (let go and let God)

Learning how and when to set healthy boundaries takes time. It is a process. As you continue your journey to find SANITY, the key is to remain cool, calm, and collected. When difficult people flip your emotional trigger, do not give in to an emotional response. Continue to depend on your growing relationship with the Lord to show you how to extend love to these people, praying for Spirit-filled guidance every step of the way. It may very well be time for you to address the *I* step in SANITY and implement boundaries. Yet no matter how convicted you may feel, it's best to remember the *S* step and your goal to not make any decisions in times of high emotional stress. Stop, step back, and pray. You are retraining yourself to respond rationally and to not react emotionally. When you respond rationally, you are in control.

When you react emotionally, others are in control, and you have lost your power. Your power comes from God, so depend on that strength and pray that He will give you the right words at the right time and that you'll be able to speak them in the right way.

When It's Time to Clearly Define Our Boundaries

If we truly want to build healthy relationships, we must become emotionally strong and take control of the things we *can* control. The well-known Serenity Prayer is good to remember at this time. The Serenity Prayer is the common name for an originally untitled prayer by the theologian Reinhold Niebuhr and adopted by Alcoholics Anonymous and other 12-step programs.

> God grant me the serenity to accept the things I cannot change, courage to change the things I can, and wisdom to know the difference.

This is the essence of Dr. Laura's "stand up or move on" theory. To accept what we cannot change is to move on, and to change what we can is to stand up. Ask God to direct your path, to give you wisdom and clear discernment for the direction you should take.

Healthy and Helpful Confrontation

All too often the very word *confrontation* makes us shake in our boots. For many of us, the past experiences we've had when addressing our concerns with difficult people have been fraught with emotional outbursts and unresolved conflict. It's easy to get lost in confrontation because even if we are calm and collected, the other people can often throw us off course with their own emotional responses. It can be a vicious cycle.

Then there are those of us who have never taken a stand, and we're fearful that to do so will cause uncomfortable conflict.

But it helps to remember this: We want to confront the *issue*—not the person. This is what we mean when we say, "Love the sinner but hate the sin."

John Townsend advises that when we are establishing a new boundary with someone, we need to be as specific and as clear as possible about the issue we want to confront. "It's important to remember there are only three things on the table: you, the other person, and the issue. Speak appropriately to each one."[1]

For many of us, learning to "speak appropriately to each one" is the crux of the matter. Learning to communicate effectively is going to be a lifelong journey for some of us, but that doesn't mean we're doomed to remain bound by uncomfortable or harmful relationships.

Revisit the section in your notebook where you wrote down the specific problems you were having with your difficult person—these are the issues you want to address, such as gossip, unreliability, habitual lateness, swearing, stealing, adultery, leaving doors unlocked, borrowing things and not returning them, and other hot-button issues.

Preparing for a Difficult Conversation

Take heed—many people make the mistake of confronting an issue with difficult people when they are smack-dab in the middle of experiencing it. In some minor instances this can work out fine, but in tougher, more serious conflicts, it might be best to stop, step back, and address the issue later. Here are two additional helpful hints:

First, distinguish between what you prefer and what's actually wrong. Before talking with people about changing their behavior, make sure you know whether what they are doing is really a bad thing (morally wrong) or just something you don't like.

And second, utilize the proven three-step method in every challenging relationship. It's a very simple plan that works well when applied consistently. To demonstrate this method, authors often use the example of a young child who refuses to listen to Mom and pick up her clothes.

Step 1: Set the boundary. Mom tells five-year-old Susie to pick up clothes from the floor.

Step 2: Give a warning. Susie ignores her, and Mom tells her there will be a consequence if she doesn't do it now. Mom does not threaten, nag, complain, or get into an emotional tug-of-war.

Step 3: Enforce the boundary with an appropriate consequence. When Susie continues to go her own way, Mom confiscates the toys Susie is playing with and continues to require Susie to pick up her clothes. Susie does not get the toys back until she has picked up her clothes even if she cries, whines, or screams. In fact, Mom may need to repeat the three-step method to address the crying, whining, and screaming.

If Mom uses this method consistently, does not get wrapped up in an emotional tug-of-war, and consistently follows up with the appropriate consequences, Susie will eventually *internalize* the experience and understand that boundaries have power and meaning. Eventually, Susie will respond to Mom without needing to have a warning and consequence every time.

ABC's Supernanny uses this method successfully. It works, but it requires commitment, fortitude, and incredible patience on the part of the parents. Mostly, it requires that the parents drastically change the way they relate to their children and set some much-needed and long-overdue boundaries.

The difficult people in most of our lives are mature adults. When most mature people are asked to do something they should do, they will do it because they care about the people who asked or because it's simply the right thing to do. However, some immature adults act like children and don't respond without a threat of consequences. Ideally, over time and with experience, the process becomes part of these difficult people, and they don't require the consequences.

Consider a group of close friends who enjoy going out to dinner and a movie once a week. Everyone meets at Helen's place at an appointed time, and they take one car. Week after week, Marsha is late, causing the group to sometimes miss dinner reservations or the start of a movie. She has a chain of excuses: "I couldn't find my car keys," or "I decided to change my clothes at the last minute and had to iron my blouse," or "My mom called, and I couldn't get her off the phone." Everyone loves Marsha, and she's great fun to be with, but they're beginning to feel disrespected and a bit angry that they all have to pay the consequence for her lateness.

The next time they meet, Marsha is again running late, so the group decides to lovingly set a boundary. They apply the *N* step in SANITY and nip her excuses in the bud. They don't want to hurt Marsha, but Marsha's actions affect the entire group, and they feel it's time to stand up and say something. Together, they agree on a boundary and consequence, and they practice and role-play before Marsha arrives. As Christians, they even pray together, asking God to give them strength to address this matter in a loving way. Helen is appointed spokesperson, with everyone in full support. Here's how it goes when Marsha shows up 25 minutes late.

"We really enjoy this time together every week, and we know it's hard for all of us to get from work to home and then here by seven, but the three of us were here tonight, just like we always are, but you're once again late. We love driving together every week because it's fun to visit in the car and it saves on gas and parking, but we really want to leave at seven, so next week if you can't make it by then, we'll head out and you can meet us at the restaurant. Does that sound okay?"

Marsha was initially taken aback but didn't take the issue seriously. They all headed out for dinner and had a lovely time. However, when Marsha showed up at 7:20 the next week, she found a note on the door of Helen's house that read, "Hope all is well and you're safe. We left at 7:00, and we're headed for the Olive Garden by the mall. See you there! Love from all of us." The note was signed by all three of her friends, and included little *x*s and *o*s and "Luv ya" sentiments.

Setting this boundary and following up with the consequence was a hard step for the friends to do, but they needed to address the animosity and tension Marsha's lateness was beginning to cause. It would be nice to say that Marsha learned her lesson and was never again late. She did at least work hard to better manage her time and arrived more often than not at seven. When she was running late, she was prepared to meet her friends at the restaurant or movie theater because she learned that if she wasn't on time, they would leave without her.

Addressing the Consequences

A consequence is quite different from a boundary. Consequences are what happen naturally when someone violates boundaries and you enforce them.

A consequence is the effect, result, or outcome of something occurring earlier, such as an action, behavior, or decision. An accident can be the consequence of reckless driving, a divorce can be the consequence of adultery, or a stiff neck may be the consequence of sitting at a computer a long time. There are consequences to virtually every action we take or don't take.

Appropriate Consequences

My son is nearing his fourth decade of life, yet he still recalls (vividly) the time when he was in grade school and I grounded him for an entire summer because he wouldn't learn his multiplication tables. In retrospect, I can see that the punishment didn't quite fit the crime.

For some of us, determining appropriate natural consequences requires more than a bit of thought. Dr. John Townsend devotes an entire chapter to this difficult task in his book *Who's Pushing Your Buttons?* As a psychologist and expert in the field of boundaries, his insight on this topic is invaluable. I especially applaud his stance on commitment and follow-through.

> There is no substitute for following through with a consequence. This is the action that makes your words have meaning and substance to your button-pusher, rather than nagging that he simply ignores and dismisses. It is when you walk your talk. There is no real rocket science to following through. It is more a matter of determining if you have the necessary support, resources, emotional wherewithal, and courage to go through with it.[2]

If we truly desire to change the dynamics of our relationships and establish healthy boundaries, we must address five needs related to consequences.

1. The need to overcome the often-paralyzing fear of consequences.

2. The need to accept that there *will* be consequences and to be willing to live with them.

3. The need to prepare for possible consequences.

4. The need to establish an appropriate natural consequence that fits the boundary.

5. The need to pray to know God's will and walk in it.

M.B.'s younger brother had been a difficult person for decades. In response to my questionnaire, M.B. wrote this:

> I was 65 years old when the problems with my younger brother escalated to out-of-control proportion. He's never been able to keep a job longer than a few months and is always asking me and other family members for money. Every other month it's something—his car payment, the electric bill, child support, or something. Year in and year out. It's not just the money—there always seems to be some major crisis or drama in his life. It doesn't seem to dawn on him that I have a life too. I spent years trying unsuccessfully to fix the situation; when he needed my help, I always came to the rescue.
>
> Someone gave me *Setting Boundaries with Your Adult Children*, and it changed my life. He wasn't my child, but at times I felt like he was. For the first time, I stopped reacting to his crisis. I stepped back and began to look at who I was in relation to my 60-year-old brother. I'd always looked at this boundary thing as selfish and self-centered, like headshrinking mumbo jumbo. But for the first time I refused to get caught up in my brother's drama and saw how I was repeating a habit I had developed when we were kids. It didn't work then, so what made me think it was going to work now? I prayed a lot and felt confident that it was time for me to stop the flow of money. When he called to tell me his auto insurance was being cancelled the next day, I was prepared to calmly and rationally tell him no—and I did. He's upset with me now, blaming me for the fact that he's driving without insurance, but that isn't my fault, no matter how many times he says it is.

M.B. is correct; it isn't his fault. But that doesn't stop his brother from blaming him. His brother is experiencing the consequences of not paying his auto insurance premium. The fact that the younger brother didn't have the money for this bill is the consequence of other choices he's made. Perhaps he budgeted poorly, lives beyond his means, gambles, won't go to work, or has an addiction that interferes with his ability to make good choices. But whatever the reasons, they are *his* issues, not his older brother's.

As you move toward confronting the difficult person in your life, prepare yourself for every consequence you can think of. Write each one down in your notebook. And most important, continue to pray for guidance concerning the steps you should take.

The Power of Prayer

When we begin to calmly and consistently set boundaries, issue warnings, and follow up with consequences, our relationships can enter rocky terrain. Although we've tried to think of every possible scenario beforehand so we can be prepared, it's hard to predict what's really going to happen. *We* might be prepared, but chances are the difficult people are not. They may rally, but they may not. In fact, difficult people may not take your boundaries or warnings very seriously in the first place, and when the consequences come, they may be thrown for a loop.

If you have reached the point of confronting your difficult person, my prayer is that you have prayed and received clear conviction. That you know beyond any doubt this is what you must do and the Lord has given you wisdom, discernment, and strength to do it. And that you are committed to praying for the difficult person—regardless of how he or she responds.

When the Right Time Comes

When you know the time has come to make some changes in the relationship with your difficult person, remember this advice from author Steve Arterburn:

The best advice for a Christian or anyone else in a bad relationship is the same: Be honest about that relationship, and communicate honestly about it. Be direct and up-front about how the relationship is making you feel, how it's affecting you psychologically, why you think it is that you're feeling and experiencing whatever things you are. Thoughtfully and thoroughly communicate all of this with the other person, taking care as you do so to be scrupulously honest about every last bit of it.

Honesty really is the best policy.

The challenge presented by being clear and honest with whomever you're sharing a bad relationship (especially if that relationship is longstanding and/or grounded in some real intimacy) is that it means you have to have clarity on whatever relational aspect has become difficult for you. You can't really communicate in plain, honest terms about something you're not clear on, in the same way you can't give a good description of a car you only glimpsed zipping by in the dark.[3]

The following tips will help you communicate in plain, honest terms.

1. Present your need to set a boundary. Do it clearly, preferably without anger and in as few words as possible. Do not justify, apologize for, or rationalize the boundary you are setting. Do not argue! Just set the boundary calmly, firmly, clearly, and respectfully.

2. At first, you will probably feel selfish, guilty, or embarrassed when you set a boundary. Do it anyway, and tell yourself you have a right to take care of yourself. Setting boundaries takes practice and determination. Don't let anxiety or low self-esteem prevent you from taking care of yourself.

3. You can't set a boundary and take care of someone else's feelings at the same time. You are not responsible for the other person's reaction to the boundary you are setting. You are responsible only for communicating the boundary in a respectful manner. If others get upset with you, that is their problem, not yours. Remember the list you developed of possible consequences. You are prepared.

4. When you set boundaries, you might be tested, especially by those

accustomed to controlling you, abusing you, or manipulating you. Plan on it, but be firm. Remember, your behavior must match the boundaries you are setting. You cannot establish a clear boundary successfully if you send a mixed message by apologizing for doing so. Be firm, clear, respectful, and consistent in your response.

5. Most people will be willing to respect your boundaries, but some will not. Be prepared to be firm about your boundaries when they are not being respected. Be prepared to follow up with appropriate consequences. If necessary, put up a wall by ending the relationship. In extreme cases, you might have to involve the police or judicial system by sending a no-contact or cease-and-desist letter or obtaining a restraining order.

Difficult Consequences and Painful Realities

In some instances, there can be serious consequences involved when you begin to establish boundaries, and I cannot stress enough your need to be prepared, consistent, and committed to your follow-through. For example, you can refuse to allow your adult children to pick up and take their children (your grandchildren) from your home while under the influence of drugs or alcohol. But you must be prepared for the consequences, including knowing your legal rights and how to execute them in this circumstance.

Here are some more examples.

If you say, "If you leave these children home alone at night while you're at the bar, I will call Child Protective Services," then you must be prepared to call CPS and be ready for the consequences.

If you say, "If you scream and swear at me again, I will quit," you must be prepared to walk out of your job and be ready for the consequences.

If you say, "If you hit me one more time, I will move out and press charges," you need to do exactly that in the event you are hit—and be ready for the consequences.

This is why consequences must be thoroughly considered beforehand. You must say what you mean and mean what you say. If you set a boundary, issue a warning, and find that the boundary is still being violated, you must consistently follow through with the appropriate consequence. Otherwise, the perpetrator will never believe that your boundary has power and meaning, and you will lose the credibility you have been trying so hard to regain.

A Painful Truth

As we put the SANITY steps into practice, we need to remember that the difficult people in our lives may not joyfully accept our change of heart. Elizabeth Brown addressed this painful truth in her book *Living Successfully with Screwed-Up People.*

> It is possible to live victoriously in relationships that are incredibly consuming, limiting, and controlling and still not lose who you are. But sometimes the obstacles are so great and the dysfunction so consuming that to stay in the relationship means the life spirit is sucked from your soul. Some relationships ravish you; they eat you alive, destroy your self-confidence, and riddle you with criticism. They require you to give up your own identity, ideas, ideals, and goals. A relationship out of control, like a disease out of control, is malignant. Sometimes the responsible thing is to leave for the sake of those under your care or for your own mental or physical health. Leaving may be the only positive option when you can no longer survive, when your self is dying.
>
> *The single most dramatic difference between healthy and toxic relationships is the amount of freedom that exists for each person to express himself or herself as an individual.*[4]

We do have the freedom to express ourselves, but it's important that we do so in a way that will bring salt and light into the situation. If a relationship has indeed reached a point where a critical line must be drawn in the sand, we must do so only after praying and being certain that we are walking in God's will. How has God spoken to us about the situation in His Word and Spirit? It's important to stop, step back, and look at situations and our roles in them with objective clarity before we confront our difficult people.

SANITY Support

1. Think about the boundaries that are being violated in your difficult relationship. What do you think is an appropriate consequence for that boundary violation?

2. It has been said that we are free to choose, but we are not free to choose the consequences. Do you think that letting the natural consequences of your difficult person's behavior run their course helps you, or does it make life harder for you? Why?

3. If the consequences seem to make life harder, is this the reason why it may be difficult for you to set and consistently carry out the consequences of your boundary violations? Write out what will be harder for you if you uphold the natural consequences of the difficult person's behavior.

Our Circles of Concern

Any relationship involves certain mutual needs, requirements, and expectations. Depending on the depth and orientation of the relationship, things like love, respect, support, and responsibility should be happening in a good, meaningful flow between two people for the relationship to be functioning well.

But it's important to understand that not all of our interpersonal relationships carry the same emotional weight. Some relationships are clearly more intimate than others and hold a higher level of priority and influence in our lives. This is as it should be.

That leads us to these questions: Are we letting difficult relationships with bosses, coworkers, or friends consume us while we ignore vital relationships in our own families? Have we placed challenging relationships with difficult people above our relationships with our own spouses? Do we honor God when we allow our in-laws to exert control over our families? Most important, is our relationship with the God who created us thriving, or is it deteriorating?

Let's talk about the relationships God has entrusted to us.

Dr. W. Oscar Thompson Jr. wrote, "The most important word in the English language, apart from proper nouns, is *relationship*."[1]

After 20 years of service as a pastor, Dr. Thompson took a teaching position at Southwestern Baptist Theological Seminary, where he taught evangelism and touched the lives of many students before his death in 1980. In his book *Concentric Circles of Concern: Seven Stages for Making Disciples*, published posthumously by the Baptist Sunday School Board in 1981, Thompson gives specific details on how a right relationship with God and with others is the critical first step in sharing the gospel. The good news does not flow from one house to the next house by following an address list, but instead through our individual relationships. Thompson explores who we are connected to through our relationships and how we can strategically reach them for the Lord.

Using seven concentric circles, Thompson shares where to place each of our relationships within these rings. In the center is self, followed in an outward direction by family, relatives, friends, acquaintances, and strangers.

He teaches us there is much to gain from being in a proper relationship first with God, then with ourselves, and finally with others. He challenges readers to mend broken fences, starting with the innermost circles of concern and working out. His book brings home the point that relationships are *key elements* in life, and God uses them (as He does everything) to accomplish His purposes. He believes that the word *relationship* provides a stem or basis from which everything else can and will grow.

Thompson shows the direct effect relationships have on our ability to display love, and he teaches us that the most effective way to witness is by walking the talk. He offers a simple plan of meeting the needs of self and close family first, then friends' needs, and then other people's needs. Our greatest need is to love and be loved.

Most important, Thompson teaches us to let the Holy Spirit guide us to fulfill our calling of loving those in our circles of concern. (This is rarely easy when a difficult person is in that circle.) He reminds us that when we became believers, we lost the right to choose whom we want to love.

Thompson's book remains a testament to his innovative method of evangelizing, and the premise has been adapted over the years in many therapeutic environments (including Christian counseling) where variations on this model of concentric circles of concern are used to explain how to best prioritize our relationships. We will use it here to help us get a better perspective on our many relationships and their priority in our lives.

While in seminary in New Orleans, Claude V. King stumbled upon Thompson's book and believed the church would greatly benefit from reading it. King, the bestselling coauthor of *Experiencing God*, began to revise and update Thompson's book and to add study guides and tips at the end of each chapter. Carrying the same title, it released in 1999.

King says that right relationships prepare us for life. If we think back on all the good events that have occurred in our lives, we can trace them to our being in proper relationships. In contrast, broken relationships are usually associated with bad memories. King goes on to say, "Behind every broken business, friendship, or home is a broken relationship."[2] If these relationships could somehow be restored, society's most complex problems would be solved. Right relationships set the conditions that eliminate these potential problems before they develop.

How to Decide What Is Right

Healthy relationships have healthy boundaries, and healthy boundaries begin with a clear sense of ourselves and our relationship to others. This in turn comes from a right relationship with God. In his book, Thompson goes even deeper by saying that we can't have a right relationship with God and then treat others adversely. And that begs the question, how are we treating the difficult people in our lives?

When challenging relationships with difficult people make our lives increasingly stressful, we need to understand where the relationships fall within our concentric circles of concern. Just as clay on a potter's wheel won't stand upright until the clay is perfectly balanced on the very center of the wheel, our relationships will be out of line until we get the core of all our relationships in the best possible shape. Then we can work our way out from there.

The Appropriate Perspective

Once we have a better feel for where our various relationships fall

within our concentric circles of concern, we can determine what interactions are appropriate for those relationships—and therein lies a significant problem for many of us.

What *is* appropriate interaction? Author and therapist Anne Katherine has a helpful response to this question in her book *Boundaries:
Where You End and I Begin.*

> How can you develop your own sense of what's appropriate?
>
> What's your orientation to the person in question? Do you
> look up, down, or across? Are you in a receiving or a giving
> role? Is your role to give or receive support?
>
> If you're looking up to a person for guidance, supervision, or
> parenting, you are not his peer. If he's your dad, minister, ther-
> apist, or boss, you are not required to parent or counsel him.
>
> If you're looking down to a person because she's a child, a cli-
> ent, or a subordinate, she is not your peer. She should not be
> counseling you. And you should not give her inappropriate
> personal information.
>
> If you're looking across to a person, she's your peer. You sup-
> port each other. You confide in each other. Giving goes both
> ways.
>
> If you're doing peer things with someone you look up or
> down to, something's wrong. A boundary is being crossed.
> Talk about it to a peer, a therapist, or someone who is bound-
> ary wise.
>
> If you're looking down or up at someone who's a peer, some-
> thing's wrong. A wife is not a subordinate. A husband is not
> a boss. Mates are equals. The relationship has lost its footing
> and needs help.
>
> If it's part of your job to support your supervisor—if you are
> a doctor's nurse, or a boss' secretary, or in some other kind
> of position that provides direct support, where's the line? It's
> appropriate to do tasks that directly influence the effectiveness

of her work. Sharpening pencils, making business phone calls, and replenishing supplies all support her professional efforts.

Getting lunch or coffee for her is a gray area. If she's so busy that she can't make the time to get lunch, you're supporting of her work by getting lunch for her. If she has the time and doesn't want to be bothered, you are not supporting her work by getting coffee or lunch for her.

Tasks that are definitely not directly supportive of her work include ordering flowers for her husband, making dinner reservations for her anniversary, getting her uniforms from the cleaners, or picking up her favorite mystery at the bookstore.

Ask yourself, does this support her work or her life? If it supports her work, it's appropriate.[3]

This sounds logical when we see it in writing, but the gray areas confound us and weigh us down when we've not been clear about our boundaries.

It's important that we know our orientation to the difficult people in our lives. Do we look up, down, or across at them?

Many of us are reasonably intelligent adults who behave responsibly, hold jobs, and contribute to society. Nonetheless, when it comes to boundary-challenged relationships and what is and isn't appropriate, many of us are like Dorothy in Oz—utterly clueless about where we are, where we're going, or how we're even going to get there.

If you're at all confused about what is appropriate in a given relationship, this is a good time to apply the *S* step in SANITY. Stop and step back to gain a better perspective on the orientation of your relationship.

Never Underestimate the Value of Prayer

In *Concentric Circles of Concern*, Dr. Thompson also shows the importance of prayer throughout the process of discipling others. As he tells stories of reconciliation and salvation, prayer becomes the backdrop of all that happened in the people's lives. He felt that being directed by the Holy Spirit through prayer was essential to the development of others. Thompson displays this idea throughout his book to help believers see that nothing can really be done outside of prayer.

I am empowered and encouraged by author Nick Harrison's words from his book *Magnificent Prayer*:

> As Christians we have a calling. We are to "shake the gates of hell" through our prayer and to further God's kingdom on earth. Both of these are done through prayer and the resulting action that follows prayer. For when these violent prayers are heard and answered by God, there comes a parting of the waters, a way for action to take place. It happens all the time. Man prays, God moves, then man moves.[4]

Life is really all about the three-part scenario Nick writes about. After endless prayer we see God move in our lives, and then it's our turn. Applying the Six Steps to SANITY helps us prepare a way for action to take place.

SANITY Support

1. What specific things are interrupting the relationship flow between you and the difficult person in your life?

2. Consult the list on the next page and write in your notebook the names of the people in each of your circles of concern.

3. In what circles do most of your difficult people reside?

Our Concentric Circles of Concern

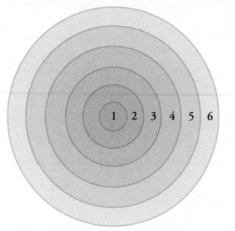

1. Center Circle of SANITY
self and our relationship with God

2. Circle of Immediate Family
spouse
children and stepchildren
parents and stepparents
siblings and step-siblings
in-laws

3. Circle of Relatives
grandparents
grandchildren
extended family

4. Circle of Close Friends
"almost like family" friends
ex-spouse
ex-in-laws
roommates

5. Circle of Acquaintances
general friends
friends of friends
bosses and employers
business partners
employees and coworkers
neighbors and landlords
clients and customers

6. Circle of the World
cashiers and vendors
customers
strangers

This diagram shows how the concentric circles of concern relate to our discussion of setting boundaries with difficult people. In the next few chapters, we'll talk about these circles and how we relate to the people in each one.

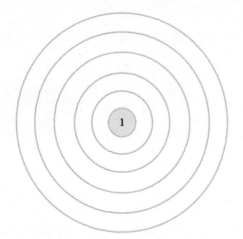

Center Circle of SANITY
self and our relationship with God

Our Center Circle of SANITY

By now, you've come to learn that setting boundaries with difficult people begins with us and our willing hearts—and we begin with God. This is the core relationship at the center of all of our relationships and our entire life.

God and us. The center circle of SANITY.

Whether in challenging relationships or healthy relationships, all Christians must acknowledge this: *We belong to God.* And that means we're precious to God. We have great worth in God's eyes—He values us.

Many of us are stuck in destructive relationship patterns. When our lives are characterized by more stress than joy, something is horribly wrong. Learning to move beyond our fear, anger, and self-defeating habits to become the people God wants us to be isn't always easy. As we practice the *Y* step in SANITY, yielding everything to God, we can feel the weight lift from our hearts as God helps us to carry the burden.

The more intimately we communicate with God, the closer we become.

Communication entails an exchange of information or opinions. It is a way to join, connect, transmit, impart, or make known. The word *communication* is derived from *communion*—a word we use to describe the Christian sacrament in which we partake of bread and wine as a commemoration of the death of Christ. *Communion* means intimate fellowship or rapport.

Ultimately, it's this intimate relationship of love that will change us, flow through us, and influence others.

We can and must deliberately choose to communicate openly with God each and every day as if our lives depended it—because they do!

Many of us talk to God in prayer—often when life is hard and we need something. But God wants to be so much more than a safe port in a storm. He wants two-way communication. In addition to hearing *from* us, He wants to talk *to* us.

God will speak to us, but we must be willing to listen.

> This doesn't mean you have to climb to the top of a mountain and lose yourself in prayer, or kneel in a church for countless hours. It just means every once in a while—while you're cooking, driving, standing in line at the bank, walking your dog, and so on—simply try opening yourself up to listening to the Holy Spirit within you. God is never *not* talking to you.[1]

Are we talking to Him? Are we stopping long enough to listen for His response?

God speaks to us through the Bible, and He uses the Holy Spirit to reveal Himself, His purposes, and His ways.

> Our experiences alone cannot be our guide. Every experience must be controlled and understood by the Scriptures. The God revealed in Scripture does not change. Throughout your life, you will have times when you want to respond based on your experiences or your wisdom. Seeking to know God's will based on circumstances alone can be misleading. This should be your guideline: Always go back to the Bible for truth (or for the Holy Spirit to reveal truth).[2]

> God speaks to individuals, and He can do it in any way He pleases. As you walk in an intimate love relationship with God, you will come to recognize His voice. You will know when God is speaking to you. He will see to it.[3]

It's almost impossible to hear God's voice when we allow ourselves to get caught up in the drama, chaos, and crisis of unhealthy relationships, when we neglect to yield everything to Him, and when we lose sight of the fact that He is our center core of life balance.

Only by moving toward Christlike maturity spiritually, mentally, and emotionally can we find inner freedom and true fulfillment. His Word teaches us, "Do not fear, for I am with you; do not be dismayed, for I am your God. I will strengthen you and help you; I will uphold you with my righteous right hand" (Isaiah 41:10).

Difficult people and challenging relationships sometimes seem to consume us like quicksand, obliterating what we know in our hearts, minds, and souls to be true. Earthly relationships can sometimes get off track, especially if our center core relationship between self and God is weak. Regardless of what is going on in our lives, God's love for us never wavers, and His Word remains steadfast and true.

Paul wrote to the Christians in Ephesus so that they might understand better the dimensions of God's eternal purpose and grace and come to appreciate the high goals God has for the church. He refers to maturity—not only doctrinal conviction and the ability to relate well to other people but also the perfectly balanced character of Christ. This is "corporate maturity" in the body of Christ.

> Christ himself gave the apostles, the prophets, the evangelists, the pastors and teachers, to equip his people for works of service, so that the body of Christ may be built up until we all reach unity in the faith and in the knowledge of the Son of God and become mature, attaining to the whole measure of the fullness of Christ.
>
> Then we will no longer be infants, tossed back and forth by the waves, and blown here and there by every wind of teaching and by the cunning and craftiness of people in their deceitful scheming. Instead, speaking the truth in love, we will grow to become in every respect the mature body of him who is the head, that is, Christ. From him the whole body, joined and held together by every supporting ligament, grows and builds itself up in love, as each part does its work (Ephesians 4:11-16).

It's time for us to do our part—to do the work required to be mature believers and supportive of our brothers and sisters in Christ.

As we look at the challenging relationships in our lives through a new lens of understanding, we must pray to make loving relationship decisions as God instructs, trusting that He will give us the strength and wisdom we need when we need it. "Those who trust in the LORD are like Mount Zion, which cannot be shaken but endures forever" (Psalm 125:1).

When difficult people consume our waking hours and threaten to drag us down to the pit of despair, it's in knowing the character of Christ that we can know how to respond to them. What matters first and foremost is the strength of our relationship with Jesus.

When we embrace our identity in God and our value to God, placing our lives and our hearts at the center of His will, only then can we begin to grasp the full measure of His love for us. From this place of right relationship, we receive the wisdom and strength to build, maintain, repair, and in some cases release the relationships in our circles of concern.

About Sin and Satan

As I live out the boundaries I've had to set in place in my own life, I'm aware that I don't always succeed as well as I'd like. Sometimes it's because of my own weaknesses, but sometimes it's from a more sinister origin: Satan and his attempts to destroy relationships.

A master of deception, Satan uses our experiences to build fortresses of lies in our thinking. Satan is first and foremost a deceiver, and we must do everything possible to remove him from power in our lives. Sin is one way Satan gains access to us. When we sin, we hand over to Satan a poisonous weapon that he will eagerly use against us. For this reason, it's critical that we strengthen our bond with the Lord Almighty, that we ask Him to reveal any sin in our lives, and that we repent accordingly, depriving Satan of this weapon.

In his book *Magnificent Prayer*, Nick Harrison refers often to our battle with the deceiver: "But praise be to God, He will not reject our prayer or withhold His love. As we depart from sin, we remove Satan's weapon and our faith is strengthened. Search yourself today and be done with any known sin."[4]

I don't know about you, but I can sometimes get hung up in life when it comes to "known" versus "unknown" sin. We know that responding in anger and disrespect toward people is a sin, even if they consistently overstep our boundaries and even if we feel they deserve it. But what about when we allow someone to violate our boundaries and we don't guard our hearts—is that a sin? When we feel anxious about a particular situation—is that a sin?

Scripture teaches us in Philippians 4:6-7, "Do not be anxious about anything, but in every situation, by prayer and petition, with thanksgiving, present your requests to God. And the peace of God, which transcends all understanding, will guard your hearts and your minds in Christ Jesus."

Not long ago I reached a point in my life where I was feeling anxious about virtually everything. An unexpected and unwanted divorce, a devastating situation with a business associate, and the heartrending betrayal of a family member that I mentioned earlier created a virtual tribulation trifecta. It proved to me that Satan had been hard at work chipping away at my self-confidence and my willingness to lay everything at the foot of the cross and trust Jesus in all things.

It was my choice to allow the anxiety and stress over the painful circumstances to take precedence over virtually everything in my life, including my time with the Lord.

I love Jesus with all my heart, and I never doubt that He has a plan for my life. But I have to say, during that time I was a horrible representative of what author Richard Stearns calls "giving others a glimpse of His love and character in all we do."

Unfortunately, I didn't always set boundaries in a loving and respectful manner with the difficult people involved. I became ashamed of that as time went by, and that shame kept me distanced from God.

It was a horrible season in my life, and I'm still feeling the consequences of setting much-needed boundaries. However, I was eventually able to release the debilitating anxiety that often propelled me to react emotionally rather than to act rationally.

I tell you this because I want you to know that my journey of understanding boundaries, repenting of my own sin, and consistently embracing my relationship with God hasn't been easy. I've cried buckets of tears the past few years, praying fervently for God to reveal His plans and His reasons for that dark and painful season in my life.

A Lightbulb Moment

I've known Thelma Wells (or Mama T, as she is lovingly known) for more than a decade, since she endorsed my first book, *God Allows U-Turns*. She is a treasured friend, and we both live in the Dallas–Fort Worth area of Texas and often see each other at local events.

A prolific author, Thelma has penned several books the past couple of years that have been mainstays on my nightstand. Filled with Post-it notes, highlighted passages, and scribbles in the margins, *Don't Give In...God Wants You to Win* and *Ready to Win over Worry and Anxiety* provided many of the tools that God knew I would need to find freedom from the weight of oppressive anxiety. But that freedom didn't come overnight. Even though I read and highlighted the transformational truth Thelma imparted, for a long time those tools remained unused in the recesses of my heart. I was too wrapped up in the drama, chaos, and crisis of my situation and circumstances to see clearly.

But one day the Holy Spirit opened the eyes of my soul, illuminating that dark place with a bondage-breaking brightness that allowed me to pick up those much-needed tools and put them to use in a powerful way. I had read these words from Thelma several times, but one day they just clicked.

> I thank God often that He's in control of everything so I have "no thing" to fear. I can honestly say that by God's grace I've learned to trust Him in such a way that worry and anxiety don't take control and run rampant in my mind and heart anymore. I've learned to give all my cares and concerns to Jesus, knowing He'll take care of me. No more oppressive anxiety

for me! Just thanksgiving for how He has given me freedom from the dreadful weight of fear. I'm not saying I never feel anxious, but that as soon as I feel even a hint of worry or anxiety, I immediately turn to Jesus for comfort, safety, and guidance. His provision in this area is part of the abundant life He came to give us![5]

It became clear to me that my anxiety itself was sin and it was time to repent. God provided what I needed when I needed it and when He knew I was ready to apply it. He also called my attention to the fact that I had forgotten to practice what I preach. I had the power to choose whether I would be wrapped up in the drama. What had I been thinking?

Sometimes we need to crawl through the anguish of life experiences to walk uprightly in the power of the Lord. Suddenly, Psalm 29:11 took on new meaning; "The LORD gives strength to his people."

Once again He would give me, a weak and wounded sinner, the strength I needed to survive. He will do the same for you.

> Knowing God does not come through a program, a study, or a method. It is the result of a vibrant, growing, one-on-one relationship with God. Within this intimate connection, God will reveal Himself, His purposes, and His ways so you can know Him in deeper and profound dimensions. As you relate to Him, God will invite you to join in His activity where He is already at work. When you obey, God accomplishes through you things only He can do. As the Lord works in and through your life, you will come to know Him ever more closely.

> Jesus said, "I have come that they may have life and have it in abundance" (John 10:10).[6]

We are a complex mix of ideas, feelings, values, wishes, perspectives, and experiences. Author Anne Katherine offers this helpful picture:

> The development of emotional boundaries and the development of self go hand in hand. Weak boundaries equal a weak self-image; a healthy self-image equals healthy boundaries.

> Boundaries without a self would be like a punctured balloon.
> It collapses when nothing is inside. A self without boundaries
> is like air without a balloon, shapeless, formless, diffused.[7]

Some of us may struggle with the emotional side effects of not setting the appropriate boundaries at the appropriate time. We may have felt unable in the past to make healthy choices in circumstances or relationships, but that doesn't mean we're doomed to continue the same course. We can jump off the gerbil wheel of insanity anytime—and into the arms of a loving Father who will never forsake us. We can overcome a great deal in life by changing the way we see God and ourselves in relationship to Him.

In her book *Seeing Yourself Through God's Eyes*, author June Hunt confirms the spiritual truth that the key to healthy Christian living is to see yourself through God's eyes. "After all," she writes, "if you don't know who you are, you cannot experience deep inner peace and complete contentment…you cannot know God's plan and purpose for your life."[8] Conversely, seeing ourselves through God's eyes opens up wonderful new possibilities. "In all these things we are more than conquerors through him who loved us" (Romans 8:37).

Boundaries are not barriers. The primary reason we need to construct them is not to keep people away, but to clearly define where we begin. And where we begin has everything to do with our personal relationship with Jesus. As we experience God in this intimate relationship, this center core reveals who we really are—whose we really are. Only then can we begin to openly communicate in love with the difficult people in our lives or know when it's time to release them.

It would be foolish to think that every challenging relationship with a difficult person can be turned around. Besides, some of the people you are dealing with may have personality disorders or mental illnesses that preclude them from healthy interaction. Bernis addresses this issue.

> It's important to understand that some difficult people have
> emotional disabilities that make it extremely difficult for them
> to relate to others in healthy ways. These emotional disabilities

create gaps in relationships that must be bridged if the relationships are going to function. The obvious problem here is that the emotionally disabled person cannot bridge that gap; therefore, if the gap is to be bridged, you will have to be the one to do it. But you cannot do that unless you are in an intimate relationship with God at the core of who you are.

Ask God to help you know when or if that gap can be bridged.

SANITY Support

1. Describe your relationship with God. Is it where it needs to be if you are going to love the difficult person in your life as God requires?

2. Do you sometimes find it difficult to know how to pray for others? Read Paul's prayers in Colossians 1:9-12; Ephesians 3:16-20; and 1 Thessalonians 5:23. How does he pray for others? Write down your answers.

3. We all deal with anxiety; it is a fact of life. But we don't have to let it rule our hearts. Is it ruling your heart? In what way does it show up in your relationships?

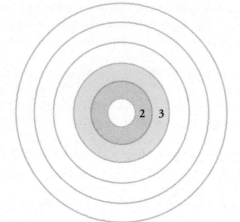

2. Circle of Immediate Family
spouse
children and stepchildren
parents and stepparents
siblings and step-siblings
in-laws

3. Circle of Relatives
grandparents
grandchildren
extended family

20

Our Circles of Immediate Family and Relatives

Having dealt with the most crucial center circle, we move to the circles of immediate family and relatives. Make no mistake, dealing with a difficult person in our immediate family can be heartrending. We hurt so much because we care so much. Bernis comments on this:

> People don't come to me for counseling when life is going well. They come for counseling when their lives have become unbearably painful. They are confused, angry, disappointed, or anxious, and they need someone to come alongside to help them renew the hope that the broken and dysfunctional relationships in their lives can be restored. But in order to do that, they must learn how to communicate, resolve conflict, and connect emotionally to one another in healthy, functional ways.

Bernis will tell you the majority of her clients are dealing with painful relationships in the second circle of concern, that of immediate family. For whatever reason, something isn't functioning properly.

What Is a Dysfunctional Family?

A dysfunctional family is one in which members suffer from fear, anger, pain, or shame that is ignored or denied.

Dysfunctional families do not acknowledge that problems exist. They don't talk about them or confront them. As a result, some family members learn to repress emotions and disregard their own needs. They become survivors. They develop behaviors that help them deny, ignore, or avoid difficult emotions. They detach themselves. They don't talk. They don't touch. They don't confront. They don't feel. They don't trust. They don't set boundaries, or they set too many. Their identities and emotional development are often inhibited. These are some of the most common challenges they face:

- a family member's addiction to drugs, alcohol, relationships, work, food, sex, or gambling

- physical, emotional, or sexual abuse

- a family member's chronic mental or physical illness

The foreword to my earlier book *Setting Boundaries with Your Aging Parents* was written by Mark Sichel, a licensed counselor and the author of *Healing from Family Rifts: Ten Steps to Finding Peace After Being Cut Off from a Family Member.* In his book, he offers this hopeful perspective:

> The unnerving news is that most of us have only very dim ideas of these dysfunctional family dynamics; few of us ever thought to question what gave rise to our own family's unique way of interacting. But there's good news, too: When you start to find out what makes your family tick—and explore your own complicity in keeping it ticking—you're on the way to a new liberation. You're en route to discovering you have a range of life-affirming choices in a realm that until now may have seemed like one in which you had few or none at all.[1]

Ah, exploring our own complicity—sometimes easier said than done, especially when the difficult people who have hurt us are in our immediate families.

My journey as the parent of a drug-addicted adult child was fraught with poor choices of my own—my own complicity. It took an extreme situation with my 35-year-old son for me to understand (with a clarity that broke my heart) the part I had been playing for years in the drama that was his life.

Things began to change when I started recognizing my own enabling patterns of behavior and learned how to finally stop accepting my son's repeated irresponsible behavior.

When I wrote *Setting Boundaries with Your Adult Children*, I never intended to write a series of books based on the topic. I wrote the book over the course of many years and out of my own pain and heartache as I managed to find SANITY in what had become an insane situation.

As I traveled the country, I began to see another equally damaging affliction threatening families—our inability (or unwillingness) to set healthy and desperately needed boundaries with our parents. People were asking difficult questions, hoping I could help them find answers. That led to the writing of *Setting Boundaries with Your Aging Parents*. But it didn't stop there. The questions continued.

"Can you tell me how to set boundaries with my husband [or wife]?"

"Will the SANITY steps help my family with my brother? He's driving us crazy."

"We live with my in-laws, and they've started to dictate how we should raise our daughter. I don't always agree with them, but my husband says to let it slide."

"My ex-wife has a new boyfriend who my kids hate. What can I say to her?"

"My husband checks my cell phone every night to see the incoming calls and grills me about numbers he doesn't recognize. It's starting to bother me. What should I do?"

What should we do?

There is no universal response to that question, but addressing the issue rationally and lovingly comes down to three things:

1. communicating in such a way that we allow the love and character of God to flow through us,

2. knowing what is and isn't our responsibility, and

3. setting firm but loving boundaries when necessary.

Mark Sichel adds this about boundaries:

> Functional families know how to create effective boundaries, ones that are not too rigid and not too fluid, and are respected but can be modified when necessary. Often the disputes that occur in families that become estranged relate to boundaries so rigid that they serve as barriers to communication of any kind, or boundaries that are so routinely invaded and overstepped that they create explosiveness, enmity, or ongoing disputes...
>
> Boundaries—whether physical, psychological or emotional—are *not* rejections. They are, in fact, ways to live harmoniously with other people in mutual respect.[2]

Mutual respect is a key phrase in every relationship scenario. Alas, difficult family relationships have existed since the beginning of time. Consider the biblical stories of Cain and Abel, Esau and Jacob, and Joseph and his brothers. In her private practice, Bernis Riley frequently addresses this topic.

> I often tell clients that difficult family relationships are nothing new. In fact, it started back in Genesis. Once sin entered the picture in chapter 3, the first thing that Adam and Eve do is to cover their shame and hide from God. Then once God's presence revealed their sin, the same man who declared "Wowman" (Adam's word for woman) at the first sight of Eve in chapter 2 now begins blaming this woman and God for the predicament he was in.
>
> The first thing we want to do when things go bad or wrong is to cover it up and hide it away. Then, when that doesn't work, we begin to blame someone else for what happened. Those are the two worst things we can do. God draws Adam and Eve out of hiding and begins to communicate openly with them about what happened. Not to assign blame or to heap shame on them, but to get them to honestly look at the situation and to bring it before Him. Nothing good will ever come of covering up, hiding, and blaming. We must risk entering into intimate communication if we are to ever come into an

understanding of one another and what goes on inside each of our hearts. But that's very scary to most people.

The Pain of Consequences

I once had an employee who consistently challenged my requests and methods. This person frequently disrespected my authority role and when confronted would often cry and become extremely emotional. Eventually this employee caused significant damage to my company by seriously overstepping boundaries and willingly participating in a triangulation—a debilitating wedge of dissension between myself and another associate.

This was an almost impossible situation from the start. At that time, the company lacked a well-defined leadership structure and a clear definition of roles and final authority. In addition, this employee was also a member of my family.

Note to self: Never hire a family member to work in a business you own.

Long story short, I trusted this person, and when things fell apart, I felt deeply betrayed.

Setting boundaries with family members can cause devastating heartache in our lives. This is especially true if we don't consistently approach problems in a way that honors God and extends love outward.

In her book *Surviving a Shark Attack (on Land)*, Dr. Laura Schlessinger writes, "When your expectations of and for people are out of whack with reality, you yourself create your own sense of hurt and betrayal."[3]

This made great sense to me as I tried to figure out how to deal with the emotional upheaval this family member caused. To say I was without fault would be untrue. In retrospect, I handled the situation poorly from the start. For the longest time, nearly all of my responses to this person were emotional. I failed miserably in responding rationally when this person overstepped boundaries, which happened often. I was unable to consistently set healthy boundaries and to exact appropriate consequences in a firm yet loving manner, and that was part of the reason for the stress and anguish that eventually brought me dangerously close to a complete nervous breakdown.

By the time I hit my breaking point and realized that enough was enough, I had lost all credibility as a leader and felt forced to take drastic measures to stop the gerbil wheel of insanity. Just as Dr. Laura wrote, I had expectations of this family member, and when those expectations were not met, I had created my own sense of hurt and betrayal.

I do believe that we have the ability to choose how we respond to people, but behaving rationally is sometimes impossible if we try to do so in our own strength.

In his book *Who's Pushing Your Buttons?* Dr. John Townsend says we must learn to be less reactive when people trigger negative feelings in us. We need to be in control of ourselves and our responses if we are to effectively help people change. This is particularly critical when our difficult people are members of our immediate families. These relationships bring years of history to the table—both good and bad.

> When you care, you are vulnerable. At the same time, however, understand this: The fact that others can affect you deeply may say some very good things about who you are. If you are able to care about someone else so much that they make you feel crazy and powerless, you have the capacity for love and attachment, and that is a wonderful thing. This capacity is one of the most important aspects of what being alive and human are all about. If you can feel, care, be vulnerable, get frustrated, love, and hate, then you are not dead inside but alive.[4]

That may be so, but it doesn't stop the pain. There is so much negative history and dysfunction in some of our immediate family relationships that it seems virtually impossible to go in and repair all the broken parts that have led to this place.

Yet nothing is impossible with God.

Prayer for wisdom and discernment is important in any relationship where boundary violations occur, yet it is critical when a difficult person falls within our second or third circles of concern. These aren't relationships that began yesterday, and the ripples of discord can have devastating effects, touching numerous people.

The majority of respondents to my questionnaire voiced concerns over relationships in their immediate family. Consider this example.

> My husband and I are currently living with his father. What started out as a good thing has become very difficult for me. I'm learning my boundaries are being crossed to the destruction of my peace and my SANITY. It's a difficult situation because I'm a people pleaser and feel tremendous guilt if I stand up for myself. I often doubt my decisions and become double minded. We are having difficulty with my eldest son, and it's been suggested that the difficulty comes from my lack of respect to the person crossing my boundaries. My self-esteem is often at a low because of the guilt I place on myself.
>
> We are currently praying about what to do with the situation.

Another person shared this about a painful relationship with a family member:

> My husband's family has always treated him like he is the red-headed stepchild, and his mother was the worst. She has since passed, but the poor treatment has not. It seems to me the only time they want anything to do with him is when they want something from him. I am polite to them when we get together for Thanksgiving and Christmas. Otherwise, I avoid them. It is very difficult for me to be in the same room with someone who is treating my husband like he is less than dirt. I have a voice and tend to use it. But for my husband's sake, in this situation, I stay quiet and stay away. This may not be the best answer, but it is the best one for me. Being family does not give a person the right to be verbally, mentally, emotionally, or physically abusive.

Susie Eller, a well-respected author and speaker, shared an example about setting a boundary with an extended family member.

> This person sent me a very hurtful and strange e-mail. It was out of the blue. It was explosive and angry, and at the end, it said, "I need you to do X and Y."

> After reading it, I realized this loved one was scared because of a situation that had come up in her own life. I responded with, "I think what you are saying is that you are scared, and I want to listen because I love you, but it's not okay to say the hurtful things that you did."
>
> There were many more e-mails. Random. Untrue and unkind. I explained one more time that I loved her and I wanted to be there for her but that what she was doing was like a stranger coming up to someone on the street and boxing them in the mouth repeatedly and then asking for help. I set gentle boundaries but left the door wide open, and I let her know that I cared about her situation.
>
> Months have passed without my extended family member talking to me.
>
> I continue to love this person, and the door is always wide open for a relationship. I can't make her talk to me—that's not my domain—but I can continue to pray and love her.

Susie handled this situation with aplomb, but not all of us are able to be as gracious—at least not in our own power, which is why we need to depend on the power of God to work through us and trust that if we come from a genuine place of authentic love for the Lord, He will bring glory from even the most devastating circumstances.

I've found that to be true in my own journey as I've suffered the pain of boundary-setting consequences and learned life-changing truth as a result.

In her book *When the Hurt Runs Deep,* Kay Arthur recounts a couple's incredible story of suffering.

> The husband had once headed up a church ministry that had been so blessed by God that it attracted national attention. But then jealousy raised its ugly head, and it all began to unravel. It reminded me of Saul's jealousy of David and his attempts to get rid of the younger man.
>
> The husband made the mistake in thinking his team could

share leadership responsibilities, without any clear definition of roles and final authority. This lack of well-defined leadership structure provided an opportunity for individuals to act on their jealousy, and a coup was carried out during the couple's direly needed sabbatical.

Everything changed overnight.

Our friend was summarily removed as pastor of the church. Not only that, but he was made to jump through all sorts of hoops, a complicated process that ate up all of the couple's savings and left them virtually penniless.

Night after night this man and his prayer-warrior wife held each other and wept, until finally they ran out of tears. Under the crushing weight of this pain, they began to understand, perhaps for the first time, the deep pain of others. As a result, they felt a compassion for suffering and disadvantaged people beyond what they had experienced before.[5]

When left to our own devices, we can often make incredibly poor choices in setting boundaries with difficult people who are also members of our family. My own story is a prime example. I wish I could turn back the clock on my situation, but the fact is that much like the couple in Kay Arthur's story, the experience has clearly changed my perspective—not only on setting boundaries but also on what it really means to depend on God and trust Him for all things.

If the challenging relationship in your life includes a family member, I encourage you to spend a great deal of time on the *S* step in SANITY—stop, step back, and pray without ceasing to gain wisdom and discernment so you can clearly understand God's will concerning how you should proceed.

SANITY Support

1. Reread the section entitled "What Is a Dysfunctional Family?" Did the family you grew up in, your family of

origin, fit the description of a dysfunctional family? If so, what was the dysfunction?

2. Does your current family fit the description of a dysfunctional family? If so what is the dysfunction?

3. Even if you are not continuing your family of origin's dysfunction, you have probably carried into your own family the dysfunctional ways you learned to cope with problems. What might be those dysfunctional ways of coping?

4. What steps do you plan to take to stop the insanity of a dysfunctional family? Write out those steps in your journal.

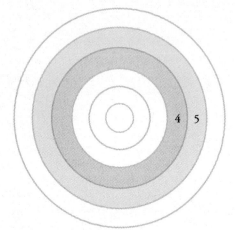

4. Circle of Close Friends
"almost like family" friends
ex-spouse
ex-in-laws
roommates

5. Circle of Acquaintances
general friends
friends of friends
bosses and employers
business partners
employees and coworkers
neighbors and landlords
clients and customers

21

Our Circles of Close
Friends and Acquaintances

These two circles of concern can represent a significant number of people and include the relationships we have at work—a place where we find ample opportunities to relate to difficult people.

Confronting people in your personal life differs from confronting people on the job. Authority and accountability structures exist at work, and policies govern what goes on there—or at least what should.

I once conducted business with a person who was my polar opposite. (Remember the chapter on temperaments?) Had we approached the business relationship with appropriate boundaries and especially defined role responsibilities, this could have been a positive experience. Unfortunately, it turned out to be quite the opposite as we both gauged the relationship based on our own motivations, perceptions, and expectations, which were quite different.

From the very start, this person overstepped boundaries and did things I felt were my responsibility. She was only trying to help, yet in many cases she didn't understand the big-picture consequences of her actions. When I spoke up, I was often perceived as the bad guy who was unwilling to release control.

Instead of embracing our unique personalities and utilizing our different gifts, we approached every boundary challenge with increasing turmoil and stress. What began as petty differences turned into cataclysmic catastrophes—all because healthy boundaries and respective role responsibilities were not clearly established from the start.

The relationship was like a ride on a roller coaster that never stopped until a firm boundary was set.

Would I do things differently today? Most assuredly. Yet I learned a great deal from the mistakes I made in that business relationship. The primary lesson was that in many life circumstances, we should get shared agreements *in writing*. Relying on individual assumptions can often result in painful consequences that can be avoided if addressed early in the relationship.

Agreeing on workable arrangements (boundaries) is useful not just in the workplace. Even with a roommate (one of the relationships in these circles), it's best to put your mutual expectations in writing first. If you accept a job, enter a business partnership, or loan money to a relative, get all of the terms and conditions in writing first. If you hire someone to do work for you, get the specifics of the task in writing first—before you provide funds for the service.

This is not being cynical or untrusting. It's being wise.

These are all logical steps to take, yet we often overlook them to the detriment of our relationships. Many challenging situations with difficult people can be avoided if we take the time to discuss and agree on specifics beforehand and not after the fact.

Compartmentalize

"This isn't about what he did to me or our marriage; it's about what he's doing to our daughter. I'm sick and tired of the way he treats her. When is he going to step up to the plate and be responsible?" My friend Cara was seething as she grabbed another nacho chip and dipped it into the spicy salsa.

My guess was that it wouldn't be anytime soon. I'd never met her ex-husband, but I believed my new friend when she confided that he'd had an affair that led to their eventual divorce. Although Cara wasn't exacting revenge or living in the past, she was clearly more than a little angry at her ex-husband and had not forgiven him for the way he treated their daughter.

In his monthly column in *O, the Oprah Magazine*, Dr. Phil McGraw responded to a letter from a woman who was divorced and trying to be a good role model for her children while she navigated a challenging relationship with her ex-husband. Here is part of what he wrote:

> You have to negotiate a new relationship with your ex. You actually have two relationships with him—one in which he is the father of your children. The first one involves a painful history of betrayal, and you need to build a fence around that pain and work on it separately until the hurt is healed. As for the second relationship, you may not like or trust your ex, but he is the only father your children will ever have. If you love your kids, and I know you do, then make it your goal to create a peaceful relationship with their father. Tell yourself, "Only by compartmentalizing my feelings can I reach a resolution about this chapter of my life while protecting my kids."[1]

The advice to compartmentalize is critical in any relationship where a person might have multiple accountabilities, such as the ex-husband who is also the father of your children, a parent who is also your employer, an ex-mother-in-law who is also the doting grandmother to your only child, or perhaps the roommate who is also your brother.

It's impossible to give examples of situations from all the relationships that fall within these two circles of concern. Yet my prayer is that by now you are able to see that regardless of the situation, if our core circle of concern is balanced, if we are in right relationship with God, we will be better equipped to respond in more loving and rational ways to people who violate our boundaries.

SANITY Support

1. Describe a time when a friendship, business partnership, or another close relationship went badly because of poor boundaries. What would you do differently now?

2. Are there people in these circles of relationship with whom you need to put healthy boundaries in place? If so, name who they are and write out what you feel about the relationships and what you need from them.

3. What do you think about the advice to compartmentalize your feelings?

6. Circle of the World
cashiers and vendors
customers
strangers

22

Our Circle of the World

When it comes to setting boundaries with people in the furthest concentric circle of concern, it's important to pray about whether you should or shouldn't say anything at all. Consider whether you need to stand up or move on. After all, you're not likely to see this person again, and you don't have a vested interest in the relationship—or do you?

Setting healthy boundaries is not about controlling every aspect of our environment, but knowing when and how we should set them as the Holy Spirit leads us and as God provides wisdom and discernment.

Therefore, setting boundaries with strangers can be just as important as setting boundaries with those in closer circles of concern. There are no accidents in God's kingdom, and we never know when our responses might have a significant impact on strangers—or when God might be using a situation or circumstance to teach us something. Remember my experience with "swearing Ted"?

As He often does, God recently gave me a perfect example for setting boundaries with a stranger.

I was having a particularly hard time concentrating on a writing project one day in my home office. I packed up my notes, resource materials, laptop—the whole kit and caboodle—and moved to my local library. This particular branch has a huge section at the back with overstuffed chairs, worktables, and floor-to-ceiling window views. It almost resembles a chic coffee shop. In fact, it has a coffee vending machine that makes vanilla cappuccino.

It was a weekday morning. School was in session, so there wasn't a lot of activity.

I'd been working a couple of hours and had built some momentum when the sound of a woman's voice startled me, followed by the voice of a man. Coming from different directions, both were talking on their cell phones—she in English and he in French.

After a few minutes of hearing far more about this woman's personal life than I cared to know, she left. But the fellow settled in to one of the overstuffed chairs and continued his conversation as though no one else existed. As his volume increased (as we all know it can do on a cell phone), so did my level of stress. I looked around for a librarian, but no luck. I also looked for a sign banning cell phones, but no luck there either. But a library is for reading, studying, and writing, not for talking on your cell phone. It's one of the few places where silence is expected, right?

Personally, I find the lack of cell phone etiquette appalling. As if I want to look for shoes while listening to a fellow shopper tell her BFF about her recent date, swearing profusely while scanning the racks for the mate to a Stuart Weitzman pump. That time, my shopping experience screeched to a halt and I simply left the store. But this time I was encamped at the library and making headway on my project. I was not ready to leave.

After a good ten minutes (yes, I looked at my watch), I got up from my chair and slowly walked over to the man. When he saw me approach, I tapped my ear with one hand to indicate that I was able to hear his conversation and quietly said, "You're voice is getting a bit loud." He nodded apologetically as I smiled and returned to my seat. When I glanced up a few minutes later, he was gone.

There was no telling how long he would have continued his conversation had I not said something. Yes, I did have the option of packing up everything and moving or leaving, but after some thought and prayer (and in light of my ongoing study of personal boundaries), I felt it was acceptable to respectfully address this boundary violation. Thankfully, things went well.

A Useful Trick

In today's society, we come in contact with many people throughout each business day. From the grocery store to the hardware store to the big-box warehouse, over the course of our lives we will cross paths with countless people who work hard for a living.

So it's no surprise when we occasionally encounter what I call RCS (rude cashier syndrome). Years ago I picked up a trick that I still use. Instead of pointing out a cashier's rudeness, I smile and say, "Wow, you must be having a bad day." A critical component in this trick is the smile and empathetic tone of voice. Being snippy or sarcastic doesn't cut it.

Face it, we've all been there. We've all had bad days when we sound less than kind. That doesn't excuse behaving rudely or disrespectfully, but sometimes a gentle word from someone who validates us can turn things around.

This trick also works to diffuse rude customers' tempers. We've all been in line when people in front of us berate cashiers for being slow, not helpful, or responsible for their bad shopping experience. There is no excuse for verbal attack. What does it say about us if we stand by and watch someone lash out at another fellow human being in such a way? It's been said that silence implies acceptance.

It's our place to exhibit God's love whenever possible, and some people are in such a place of pain and stress, they inappropriately vent their frustration—quite often at the expense of cashiers who are only trying to do their job (a job that often requires they stand on their feet all day and deal with rude customers).

As we deal with people who enter our circle of the world, it's important to remember that we may be the only face of God they see that day.

SANITY Support

1. What is your typical response to difficult people in this

circle? Do you ignore them, do you point out their behavior, or do you treat them gently as you make your point?

2. You may be the only face of God people in this circle may see today. What impression do you want them to have of who God is?

23

Before We Go, Just Say No!

We've already discussed saying no to enabling, anger, emotional responses, and such. As you get a better handle on how to approach the challenging relationships in your life and confront difficult people, there are a few more tips I'd like to share. These are specific things you can say no to in order to guard your heart and be the vessel of love and empathy God desires for you to be.

Just Say No to Negative Influences

Bad company corrupts good character. Stay away from people who display questionable values and low moral character unless God gives you very specific conviction that He has sent you to help change their lives.

Just Say No to E-mailing and Texting Your Boundaries

When speaking with difficult people, the content of our message (what we say) and our tone of voice (how we say it) go hand in hand. No matter how unnerving it might be, the best possible way to do this is in person or on the phone.

In the retrospective wisdom that comes from having made monumental mistakes, I've learned to resist the temptation to set boundaries with difficult people using e-mail or text messages. Regardless of how well-intentioned your motives may be, it is impossible to convey a sincere tone of voice in either of these methods—if indeed you are sincere.

Remember that business associate I mentioned earlier? Eventually, our primary method of communication became e-mail and letters. Yet regardless of what I said or how I said it, without actually hearing the tone of my emotions, she often misunderstood the content of my written communication and distorted my intentions. Over the course of many months I sought the advice of several godly people, including a well-respected Christian couple who could see and hear the anguish I was going through. For some reason, those feelings did not translate through e-mail or letters to my business associate.

This kind of misconstrued intention occurs more and more as we rely on electronic communication to take the place of personal relationship.

Just Say No to Lengthy Explanations

This can be a killer. In our sincere desire to be heard, we can overexplain our feelings and perceptions. When setting boundaries, we need to do so clearly and without unnecessary embellishment or justification for the action.

Just Say No to Third-Party Triangulation

Far more often than we realize, the addition of a well-meaning individual can make an already bad situation even worse, especially if the person is an enabler or is codependent. Unless we have reached the painful place where legal counsel must intervene, the intrusion of a third person can do significant damage to a relationship with a difficult person. Bernis offers this advice:

> There are times when it is necessary to bring in a third party in order to enforce our boundaries or protect our rights. However, we often bring in an emotionally biased third party just to reduce the anxiety between us and the difficult person. This is referred to as *triangulation* and can be quite damaging in a relationship with a difficult person.

Resist the urge to be a third party or to bring in a third party. It is destined to be a no-win situation, and over time the issues will become increasingly cloudy, convoluted, and potentially critical.

Just Say No to Idle Threats

Before you set a new boundary, give advance warning to the person that it may be coming. Sometimes, the warning itself can help change behavior. The person may be unaware of how serious the problem is and of your willingness to entertain consequences. However, your difficult person may see the warning as meaningless and not respond or ignore you completely. In that case, you must be prepared to act and follow up with the appropriate consequences.

When it comes to setting healthy boundaries, it is imperative that you say what you mean and mean what you say.

Just Say No to Lack of Planning and Forethought

A number of years ago I had a career as a professional fundraising executive, and a significant part of my job was to assist board members and nonprofit organizations in the development and implementation of detailed strategic plans. I frequently conducted board retreats and planning workshops to identify and troubleshoot dysfunction within organizations, helping groups and individuals establish detailed plans and develop systems to better equip their organization to succeed.

Today, with the retrospective wisdom that comes from having walked the rough terrain of unhealthy boundaries, and having experienced the freedom of setting boundaries and finding SANITY, I can see the value of synthesizing planning into our lives as children of God who desire to stop the insanity and find balance.

It's really called holding ourselves accountable.

Parents and grandparents around the world have told me one of the most powerful and helpful exercises in *Setting Boundaries with Your Adult Children* is the instruction to write out a detailed action plan regarding the new boundaries they were setting. Likewise, the chapter in *Setting Boundaries with Your Aging Parents* where I encourage adult children to write out a script and practice what they're going to say to their toxic parents also seems to be very helpful. Writing is healing. Over the years I've heard comments like these:

- "It took my husband and me several drafts to finally get on

the same page and clearly identify the negative behavior
we were no longer going to tolerate in our home, the
limits we needed to establish, and the consequences we
were willing to carry out. Developing a written action
plan changed our lives."

- "Preparing myself ahead of time made all the difference in
the world when I told my mom that I would no longer
cover her checking account overdrafts that resulted from
her undisciplined debit-card use at a nearby casino. It was
a difficult conversation with a difficult person, but I was
proud of myself when it was over, and I think God was
too. I managed to stay calm and come from a place of love,
not anger. Practicing ahead of time made all the difference
in the world."

Role-playing isn't new, and countless professionals have used it in
some form or another for years.

I hope you've been recording your thoughts, goals, and progress in
a notebook since we began this journey together. Never underestimate
the power of putting your thoughts in writing, if for no other reason
than to hold yourself accountable on your journey.

Just Say No to Always Saying Yes

Here's a good rule to implement: Never say yes to anything without
taking time to think it through. Remember the *S* step in SANITY—
stop, step back, and pray.

For example, let's say your mother calls and wants you to take her
to a doctor appointment tomorrow afternoon. This isn't unusual—she
frequently calls at the last minute and usually makes you feel guilty
and adds stress to your already stress-filled life. So this time, instead of
saying yes, tell her you will look at your calendar and get back to her.
You may know perfectly well you have the time and are willing to take
her, but put her off a few hours before you agree to do it. This does
two things. It tells her that you have a schedule you need to consider

and that you cannot be expected to automatically say yes to her every request. It also tells her you have a life separate from hers. If you actually do have something planned tomorrow afternoon, ask her about the urgency of the appointment. If it is not vital, offer to take her another time. If it is urgent, discuss other transportation options.

Will you feel guilty telling her no? Probably, but get over it. Will she be upset with you because you won't change your plans? Probably, but she'll get over it. Remember, you are not rejecting your mother. You're only saying no to her request.

This example illustrates a classic one-liner: Stress is what happens when your insides are saying, "No, I can't do this," and your mouth is saying, "Yes, of course I would be happy to."

Just Say No to Drug and Alcohol Addictions

Since *Setting Boundaries with Your Adult Children* released, I have spoken with many parents who are dealing with drug- and/or alcohol-addicted adult children. These parents have seen their kids in and out of rehabilitation centers, jail, and prison. They've watched them go through numerous jobs and marriages, and they've exhausted their emotional and financial resources trying to help them. Many of these parents have spent years trying to better understand where their adult children are coming from, but they're still at a loss.

If parents seriously want to get off the catastrophe carousel, they must learn how their responses and their choices have contributed to this dysfunctional dynamic. Even more important, they must change.

Ultimately, the change in their responses may influence their loved ones the most.

Just Say No to Perfection

People with low self-esteem often have an irrational need for their most intimate relationships to be perfect. Consequently, they compete for control so they can make their relationships be the way they think they should be. As a result, the relationships deteriorate and become vacuous, leaving people with deep resentments and hurts. The partners find that they resent the others because they believe that after giving and giving and giving, they have nothing left of themselves to keep the relationships alive and well.

Just Say No to Intrusive Opinions

One of the most overstepped psychological boundaries has to do with the never-ending flow of popular opinion. Opinions are good things to have. Healthy communication is based on a back-and-forth flow of opinions, and we need to accept that our opinions aren't the only ones that matter. Yet it's important to have discernment when listening to opinions, as this comment from an editorial suggests.

> We live in an era in which it is important to have opinions. Not necessarily smart or original ones; almost any opinion will do as long as it's forcefully expressed. When it comes to opinions, we're all living in an intellectual Costco, where it's volume, volume, volume.
>
> It wasn't that long ago that opinions were something carefully considered and weighed, so that they'd stand the test of time and reflect well on the author. Thinkers were like gourmet chefs laboring over an elaborate meal they wanted to be perfect. But today, opinions are like Big Macs—thrown together hastily, served by the billions and not very good for you.[1]

Just Say No to Comparisons

So much about setting healthy boundaries concerns our self-esteem—or lack thereof. We are miles ahead of the pack when we can begin to look at the relationships God places in our lives as precious stepping-stone gifts that He gives us to draw us closer to Him, and not as comparisons to judge ourselves harshly. There will always be someone smarter, wittier, and more educated, but there will never be another you.

Just Say No to Crazy-Making People

We know that some people and some relationships are accidents waiting to happen, yet we continue to live the very definition of insanity with these people, repeating the same behavior over and again and expecting different results. Some people are, quite simply, what author David Hawkins calls *crazymakers*.

What does it take for us to realize that having toxic, stress-filled relationships is not how God wants us to live? That loving our neighbor does not mean allowing someone to abuse or mistreat us?

As we learn to just say no, let's also remember that God sees the whole picture of our lives—past, present, and future. And as June Hunt writes, "Discovering God's will is scroll-like. He unrolls the scroll one line at a time."[2] He says, "I will instruct you and teach you in the way you should go; I will counsel you with my loving eye on you" (Psalm 32:8).

SANITY Steps

1. What do you need to say no to? List every no you need to say.

2. As you look over this list of everything you need to say no to, which of these things do you need to do first? Which one would come next? Go through your list and put these things in order from most important to least important.

24

In Closing...

Being able to set healthy boundaries and communicate openly and honestly while being loving, kind, and direct is a sign of maturity and wisdom. In our casual relationships as well as those in the more intimate circles, God calls us always to be salt and light. My prayer is that by now you have grasped the vision for how the six steps to SANITY can make a tremendous difference in your relationships and your life.

As you become more in tune to situations that call for you to establish healthy boundaries, and as you learn to address these issues in a loving way, this rhythm of response will become increasingly natural. Working out challenging relationship issues requires honesty and courage. The more you commit to making positive changes in your responses, the better you will get. Eventually, it will become second nature.

It may take years to heal the damage created by violated boundaries in your life. You may need the guidance of a Christian counselor or therapist who can provide help. Therapist and author Anne Katherine explains.

> Even though we've spent 24 hours a day for 30 or 40 years feeling unsafe in a dysfunctional family, it takes only an hour or two of therapy a week for maybe six or seven years to heal the damage. Perhaps that sounds like a lot of therapy to you, but

what you get in exchange is immeasurable—a new life, grati-
fying relationships, and confidence in your own being.[1]

To be confident in our own being—what peace and joy that would
bring! I hope you've learned that our confidence in dealing with anything in life comes from knowing our identity in Christ and from the
relationship we have with the Almighty, not from the relationships
we have with difficult people who are disrupting our lives. How we
respond to these people will change when we ourselves are changed.

We often suffer consequences because we refuse to walk the talk—
we don't live in abundant blessings because we aren't walking the way
the Lord calls us to walk. Mature believers understand the need to please
God, and being in the Word is the only way to learn what pleases Him.

Boundaries enable us to love others with wisdom. Loving with wisdom means we order our behaviors and temper our emotions according to what is best for others. Setting healthy boundaries with difficult
people is loving them with wisdom because we are helping them do
what they cannot or will not do for themselves.

Pray for God to do a miracle in your life concerning the challenging
relationship you have with a difficult person so that you can demonstrate God's love through your actions. Author Richard Stearns offers
this perspective:

> Christianity is a faith that was meant to spread—but not
> through coercion. God's love was intended to be demonstrated,
> not dictated. Our job is not to manipulate or induce others to
> agree with us or to leave their religion and embrace Christian-
> ity. Our charge is to both proclaim and embody the gospel so
> that others can see, hear, and feel God's love in tangible ways.
> When we are living out our faith with integrity and compas-
> sion in the world, God can use us to give others a glimpse of
> His love and character. It is God—not us—who works in the
> hearts of men and women to forgive and redeem. Coercion is
> not necessary or even particularly helpful. God is responsible
> for the harvest—but we *must* plant, water, and cultivate seeds.[2]

It takes transformed people to transform the world.

As we cultivate the seed of love God has placed in our hearts, I pray that every difficult person in your life becomes nourishment to that seed. May each challenging relationship help you learn what it means to guard your heart so that what comes from it is an outpouring of love—influencing your difficult person in a positive way and enabling you to become the person God has called you to be, and in so doing, transforming your life and the world.

> Stand firm then, with the belt of truth buckled around your waist, with the breastplate of righteousness in place, and with your feet fitted with the readiness that comes from the gospel of peace. In addition to all this, take up the shield of faith, with which you can extinguish all the flaming arrows of the evil one. Take the helmet of salvation and the sword of the Spirit, which is the word of God.
>
> And pray in the Spirit on all occasions with all kinds of prayers and requests. With this in mind, be alert and always keep on praying for all the Lord's people (Ephesians 6:14-18).

Sample Letters

To a Difficult Ex-Spouse

Dear _____,

I realize that since our marriage ended, things between us have been hard. I also realize that I've said and done some things that have hurt your feelings and have damaged our relationship. I want you to know that I'm sorry for hurting you and causing harm to our relationship. I want things to change between us, and though I desire that we both change, I cannot make you change. I can only change myself and my responses and reactions to you, so I'm choosing to set some boundaries for the health of this relationship.

From now on, rather than withdrawing from you or attacking you when I feel criticized by you, I will simply let you know that your words have hurt my feelings, and I will ask you to acknowledge my hurt feelings and take back the hurtful words. If you cannot do this, I will not continue that conversation with you. Until you acknowledge the hurtful words or actions, any communication between us will be limited to only what is necessary for exchanging information. In other words, just the facts, nothing more, nothing less.

In addition, you are required to follow the judge's ruling in our divorce papers, and if you choose not to abide by that legal document, I will notify my lawyer, and the legal system will enforce those rulings. I sincerely want a good and respectable relationship between us, so that is why I am letting you know what my boundaries are from this time forward.

Sincerely,

_____ Date _____

To a Coworker or Boss

Dear _____,

I want to have a good working relationship with you, and I believe you want the same with me. However, I feel that in order to have a good working relationship with you, I need to let you know that there have been several times in the past few weeks [or months] that you have crossed what I consider to be personal or professional boundaries with me. For instance, [state a couple of examples to illustrate your point].

In order to work effectively with you I will not allow boundaries like these to be crossed in the future. If you do continue to violate my personal or professional boundaries, I will find it necessary to file a complaint with Human Resources [or the person's immediate boss]. I would like to speak with you personally about this letter so that I'm not misunderstood and so that you can be clear about what I need from you in the future. I would like to arrange a meeting between us and [another coworker or boss] to discuss this issue.

Thank you,

_____ Date _____

To a Difficult Family Member

Dear _____,

I want you to know how important you are to me. I highly value our relationship and want it to be the best it can be.

However, over the past few years [or months], some things

have happened between us that I feel have damaged our relationship. [Name a few of those things.] I don't want these things to come between us and hinder our relationship, but neither can I sit quietly by and not say anything. In the past, I've felt powerless to say anything, but now I realize that you're much too important in my life for me to not try to mend our relationship. I need you to understand that I do not hold these things from the past against you, but should something like this happen again, I will _____.
[Write your boundary and its consequence. For example, "I will immediately end our conversation if you start calling me names, and I will not have contact with you until you apologize."] We both are responsible for the health of this relationship, and this is what I must do to take my part of that responsibility.

Sincerely,

_____ Date _____

To a Difficult Friend

Dear _____,

I want you to understand that I write this letter with great difficulty. Our friendship has meant a great deal to me over the years, and the last thing I want to do is to ruin it. However, some things have recently happened that have me wondering if we can continue to be friends as we once were. I need you to know up front what some of those things are so you're not wondering about them. [Name the things your friend has done that have harmed you during the friendship.] I don't think you intentionally wanted to hurt me, but I need you to know that those things did hurt me and made me to want to pull away from our friendship.

So in the future, if you [name the offense], I will call your attention to it and will ask you to take responsibility for your behavior. If you cannot do that, I will need to back away from

this relationship for my own well-being. I hope you understand that I want to rebuild this relationship into a safe friendship for both of us.

Your friend,

_____ Date _____

To End a Relationship with a Difficult Family Member or Friend

Dear_____,

I've been thinking about our relationship lately and have come
to realize that perhaps the best thing for both of us would
be for us to discontinue our contact with each other until
you have [apologized for..., admitted..., begun counseling,
stopped drinking...]. For my own well-being and that of my
[family, children, parents], I'm willing to let this relationship
go. We both need to make some changes for the better, but I
can't do that as long as this relationship is in its present state.

I don't know if you will care that I am taking this step or not.
All I know is that I need to do this for my own sanity and
because I do care about you.

Sincerely,

_____ Date_____

A FINAL NOTE FROM ALLISON

TO GET SANITY SUPPORT

We'll soon be launching new SANITY Support Group programs and services, designed to equip you with the tools needed to live a life of freedom—to experience the hope and healing that comes from clearly defining where you stop and another begins.

My prayer has always been to offer support to men and women addressing the myriad issues that swirl around the central core of unhealthy boundaries, such as adult children, aging parents, difficult people, teens, food, and other topics.

To find out if a Six-Step SANITY Support Group may be meeting in your neighborhood, or for guidelines how to begin your own SANITY Support Group, visit our website at:

SettingBoundariesBooks.com

Notes

Introduction

1. Elizabeth B. Brown, *Living Successfully with Screwed-Up People* (Grand Rapids, MI: Revell, 2010), 16.

Chapter 1: Keeping Your Eye on the Goal

1. Laura Schlessinger, *Surviving a Shark Attack (on Land): Overcoming Betrayal and Dealing with Revenge* (New York, NY: HarperCollins, 2011), 108.

2. Karol Ladd, *A Woman's Passionate Pursuit of God* (Eugene, OR: Harvest House, 2011), 16.

3. Ladd, *A Woman's Passionate Pursuit*, 19.

Chapter 2: Understanding Boundaries

1. Henry Cloud and John Townsend, *Boundaries: When to Say Yes, When to Say No to Take Control of Your Life* (Grand Rapids, MI: Zondervan, 1992), 276.

2. Cloud and Townsend, *Boundaries*, 25.

3. Anne Katherine, *Boundaries: Where You End and I Begin* (Center City, MN: Hazelden Foundation, 1991), 131.

Chapter 3: Embracing the Most Important Relationship

1. Stephen Arterburn and John Shore, *Being Christian: Exploring Where You, God, and Life Connect* (Bloomington, MN: Bethany House, 2008), 35.

2. Richard Stearns, *The Hole in Our Gospel: What Does God Expect of Us? The Answer That Changed My Life and Might Just Change the World* (Nashville, TN: Thomas Nelson, 2009), 73-74.

3. Retrieved from www.allaboutgod.com/love-thy-neighbor.htm.

Chapter 4: Identifying Core Challenges

1. John Townsend, *Who's Pushing Your Buttons? Handling the Difficult People in Your Life* (Nashville, TN: Thomas Nelson, 2004), 28.

2. Allison Bottke, *Setting Boundaries with Your Adult Children: Six Steps to Hope and Healing for Struggling Parents* (Eugene, OR: Harvest House, 2008), 28-29.

3. Laura Schlessinger, *Bad Childhood, Good Life: How to Blossom and Thrive in Spite of an Unhappy Childhood* (New York, NY: HarperCollins, 2006), 7.

4. Townsend, *Who's Pushing Your Buttons?* 27.

Chapter 5: Addressing Emotions
1. Townsend, *Who's Pushing Your Buttons?* 12-13.

Chapter 6: Tracking the Temperaments
1. Florence Littauer, *Personality Plus: How to Understand Others by Understanding Yourself* (Grand Rapids, MI: Fleming H. Revell, 1983), 11.

Chapter 7: Confronting Anger
1. Harriet Lerner, *The Dance of Anger: A Woman's Guide to Changing the Patterns of Intimate Relationships* (New York, NY: HarperCollins, 2005), 9-10.

2. Lerner, *The Dance of Anger*, 44.

3. June Hunt, *Counseling Through Your Bible: Providing Biblical Hope and Practical Help for 50 Everyday Problems* (Eugene, OR: Harvest House, 2008), 53.

Chapter 8: Choosing to Change
1. Schlessinger, *Bad Childhood, Good Life*, 2.

2. Schlessinger, *Bad Childhood Good Life*, 23-24.

3. David Hawkins, *Dealing with the CrazyMakers in Your Life: Setting Boundaries on Unhealthy Relationships* (Eugene, OR: Harvest House, 2007), 205.

4. Mark Sichel, *Healing from Family Rifts: Ten Steps to Finding Peace After Being Cut Off from a Family Member* (New York, NY: McGraw-Hill, 2004), 118.

5. John Townsend, *Handling Difficult People: What to Do When People Try to Push Your Buttons* (Franklin, TN: Integrity House, 2006), 16.

6. Stormie Omartian, *Stormie: A Story of Forgiveness and Healing* (Eugene, OR: Harvest House, 1998).

7. Stearns, *The Hole in Our Gospel*, 243-44.

Chapter 9: Moving Forward with Purpose
1. Arterburn and Shore, *Being Christian*, 101-2.

Chapter 10: The Power of SANITY
1. Stearns, *The Hole in Our Gospel*, 245.

Chapter 11: *Stop* Your Own Negative Behavior and Destructive Patterns
1. Leslie Vernick, *The Emotionally Destructive Relationship: Seeing It, Stopping It, Surviving It* (Eugene, OR: Harvest House, 2007), 119-20.

2. Bottke, *Setting Boundaries with Your Adult Children*, 105.

3. Bottke, *Setting Boundaries with Your Adult Children*, 106-7.

4. Henry T. Blackaby and Claude V. King, *Experiencing God: How to Live the Full Adventure of Knowing and Doing the Will of God* (Nashville, TN: Broadman & Holman, 1994), 31.

Chapter 12: *Assemble* a Support Group

1. *NIV Woman's Devotional Bible* (Grand Rapids, MI: Zondervan, 1990), 1394.

Chapter 13: *Nip* Excuses in the Bud

1. Hawkins, *Dealing with the CrazyMakers in Your Life*, 26.
2. Cloud and Townsend, *Boundaries*, 228.
3. June Hunt, *Seeing Yourself Through God's Eyes: A 31-Day Devotional Guide* (Eugene, OR: Harvest House, 2008), 61.

Chapter 14: *Implement* Rules and Boundaries

1. Cloud and Townsend, *Boundaries*, 100.

Chapter 16: *Yield* Everything to God

1. Vernick, *The Emotionally Destructive Relationship*, 197.
2. Vernick, *The Emotionally Destructive Relationship*, 198.

Chapter 17: How to Practice SANITY

1. Henry Cloud and John Townsend, *How to Have That Difficult Conversation You've Been Avoiding: With Your Spouse, Adult Child, Boss, Coworker, Best Friend, Parent, or Someone You're Dating* (Grand Rapids, MI: Zondervan, 2005), 139.
2. Townsend, *Who's Pushing Your Buttons?*, 155.
3. Arterburn and Shore, *Being Christian*, 100-101.
4. Brown, *Living Successfully with Screwed-Up People*, 56.

Chapter 18: Our Circles of Concern

1. W. Oscar Thompson Jr. with Carolyn Thompson Ritzmann, *Concentric Circles of Concern: Seven Stages for Making Disciples,* revised and updated by Claude V. King (Nashville, TN: Broadman & Holman, 1999), 8.
2. In Thompson with Ritzmann, *Concentric Circles of Concern*, 10.
3. Katherine, *Boundaries*, 96-97.
4. Nick Harrison, *Magnificent Prayer: 366 Devotions to Deepen Your Prayer Experience* (Grand Rapids, MI: Zondervan, 2001), 116.

Chapter 19: Our Center Circle of SANITY

1. Arterburn and Shore, *Being Christian*, 36-37.
2. Blackaby and King, *Experiencing God*, 223-24.
3. Blackaby and King, *Experiencing God*, 194.
4. Harrison, *Magnificent Prayer*, 67-68.
5. Thelma Wells, *Ready to Win over Worry and Anxiety* (Eugene, OR: Harvest House, 2010), 49.
6. Blackaby and King, *Experiencing God*, 2.
7. Katherine, *Boundaries*, 70.
8. Hunt, *Seeing Yourself Through God's Eyes*, 9.

Chapter 20: Our Circles of Immediate Family and Relatives

1. Sichel, *Healing from Family Rifts*, 41.

2. Sichel, *Healing from Family Rifts*, 81.

3. Schlessinger, *Surviving a Shark Attack (on Land)*, 81.

4. Townsend, *Who's Pushing Your Buttons?*, xxiv.

5. Kay Arthur, *When the Hurt Runs Deep: Healing and Hope for Life's Desperate Moments* (Colorado Springs, CO: WaterBrook Press, 2010), 103-4.

Chapter 21: Our Circles of Close Friends and Acquaintances

1. Phillip C. McGraw, *O, the Oprah Magazine*, November 2009, 68-70.

Chapter 23: Before We Go, Just Say No!

1. Stephen Randall, "Mouthing Off in America," *Los Angeles Times*, January 16, 2011, Op-Ed.

2. Hunt, *Counseling Through Your Bible*, 116.

Chapter 24: In Closing …

1. Katherine, *Boundaries*, 121.

2. Stearns, *The Hole in Our Gospel*, 18.

Coming Soon from Allison Bottke and Harvest House Publishers…

Setting Boundaries™ with Food

We can "just say no" to enabling our adult children, or to allowing difficult people to control us. Yet it's impossible to "just say no" to food—for without it we would die. Allison Bottke struggled for years with overeating and being overweight, but then she lost 120 pounds after having weight loss surgery. However, the journey to her true weight loss freedom came in the years after surgery, when she discovered the connection between healthy boundaries and successful long-term weight loss.

"Carrying extra weight provides many of us with a false sense of safety—protection—it's a good way to keep people at a distance. Attending to our heart is an important part of changing the outside. Setting boundaries with food and finding SANITY from the vicious cycle of dieting can help you find freedom at last."

*Before setting
boundaries with food*

*After setting
boundaries with food*

Also available from Allison Bottke
and Harvest House Publishers...

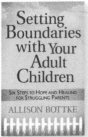

Setting Boundaries™ with Your Adult Children:
Six Steps to Hope and Healing for Struggling Parents

This important and compassionate book (more than 80,000 copies sold) from the creator of the successful *God Allows U-Turns* series offers help if your adult children continue to make life painful for you.

Writing from firsthand experience, Allison identifies the lies that kept her and her son in bondage—and how she overcame them. Additional real life stories from other parents are woven through the text.

A tough-love book to help you cope with dysfunctional adult children, *Setting Boundaries™ with Your Adult Children* will empower your family by offering hope and healing through SANITY—a six-step program to help you regain control in your home and in your life.

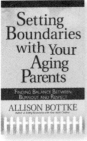

Setting Boundaries™ with Your Aging Parents:
Finding Balance Between Burnout and Respect

This important book provides help if you long for a better relationship with your parents but feel trapped in a never-ending cycle of chaos, crisis, or drama.

With keen insight and a passion to empower adult children, Allison charts a trustworthy roadmap through the often unfamiliar territory of setting boundaries with parents while maintaining personal balance and avoiding burnout. Through the use of professional advice, true stories, and scriptural truth, you will learn how to apply the Six Steps to SANITY.

About Allison Bottke

Allison Bottke is a bestselling inspirational author, speaker, and the founder of the acclaimed *God Allows U-Turns*® book series and outreach ministry. She is the author or editor of more than 25 nonfiction and fiction books. Visit AllisonBottke.com or SettingBoundariesBooks.com. E-mail Allison at Allison@AllisonBottke.com.

To learn more about Harvest House books and
to read sample chapters, log on to our website:

www.harvesthousepublishers.com

HARVEST HOUSE PUBLISHERS
EUGENE, OREGON